statutes Great Britain. Laws

The Indian Council Acts

1861 and 1892

statutes Great Britain. Laws

The Indian Council Acts
1861 and 1892

ISBN/EAN: 9783744666862

Printed in Europe, USA, Canada, Australia, Japan

Cover: Foto ©ninafisch / pixelio.de

More available books at **www.hansebooks.com**

THE

INDIAN COUNCILS ACT,

AND THE

ACTS AMENDING IT

WITH

ALL OFFICIAL PAPERS CONNECTED THEREWITH AND THE RULES FOR THE CONDUCT OF BUSINESS.

AT

MEETINGS OF THE COUNCIL.

Madras:

PRINTED AT THE NATIONAL PRESS,
100, MOUNT ROAD.

1893.

Price One Rupee.

PREFACE.

The Acts, Rules and utterances having a bearing on the subject of the Reconstitution of the Legislative Councils in this country are collected together in the following pages to facilitate reference in the coming years when, the discussion is bound to go on, having regard to the really inadequate and reluctant response that has been vouchsafed to the earnest appeal, for a period of eight years, on the part of the Indian National Congress.

M. V.

15th May
1893.

TABLE OF CONTENTS.

———:o:———

	Page.
The Indian Councils Act (1892)	1
The Indian Councils Act (1861)	5
Act of 1869 amending the Indian Councils Act of 1861.	20a
Act of 1870 ,, ,, ,, ...	20b
Act of 1871 ,, ,, ,, ...	20d
Memorandum by the British Committee of the Indian National Congress on the Act with Extracts from the speeches of Responsible Statesmen in England	21
His Excellency Lord Lansdowne's speech on the Rules under the Indian Councils Act (1892)	42
His Excellency Lord Lansdowne's speech on the Constitution of Legislative Councils	47
Rules regarding the constitution of the Legislative Council	57
Regulations under Section I (4) for Madras	58
,, ,, for Bombay	60
,, ,, for Bengal	62
,, ,, for the N.-W. Provinces and Oudh	64
Rules relating to the nomination of members to the Legislative Councils of Bengal	66
,, ,, ... Bombay	73
,, ,, ... Madras	76
,, ,, ... N.-W. Provinces & Oudh.	79
Correspondence between the Government of India and the Right Honorable the Secretary of State ...	81
Rules for the Conduct of Business at Meetings of the Council of the Fort St. George	95

THE INDIAN COUNCILS ACT (1892.)

An Act to amend the Indian Councils Act, 1861.

20*th June,* 1892.

BE it enacted by the Queen's Most Excellent Majesty, by and with the advice and consent of the Lords Spiritual and Temporal, and Commons, in this present Parliament assembled, and by the authority of the same, as follows :—

1. (1) The number of additional members of Council nominated by the Governor-General under the provisions of section ten of the Indian Councils Act, 1861, shall be such as to him may seem from time to time expedient, but shall not be less than ten nor more than sixteen ; and the number of additional members of Council nominated by the Governors of the presidencies of Fort St. George and Bombay respectively under the provisions of section twenty-nine of the Indian Councils Act, 1861, shall (besides the Advocate-General of the presidency or officer acting in that capacity) be such as to the said Governors respectively may seem from time to time expedient, but shall not be less than eight nor more than twenty. _{Provisions for increase of number of members of Indian Councils for making laws and regulations. 24 & 25 Vict, c. 67.}

(2) It shall be lawful for the Governor-General in Council by proclamation from time to time to increase the number of Councillors whom the Lieutenant-Governors of the Bengal Division of the presidency of Fort William and of the North-Western Provinces and Oudh respectively may nominate for their assistance in making laws and regulations : Provided always that not more than twenty shall be nominated for the Bengal Division, and not more than fifteen for the North-Western Provinces and Oudh.

(3) Any person resident in India may be nominated an additional member of Council under sections ten and twenty-nine of the Indian Councils Act, 1861, and this Act, or a member of the Council of the Lieutenant-Governor of any province to which the provisions of the Indian Councils Act, 1861, touching the making of laws and regulations, have been or are hereafter extended or made applicable.

(4) The Governor-General in Council may from time to time with the approval of the Secretary of State in Council, make regu-

lations as to the conditions under which such nominations, or any of them, shall be made by the Governor-General, Governors, and Lieutenant-Governors, respectively, and prescribe the manner in which such regulations shall be carried into effect.

Modification of provisions of 24 & 25 Vict, c. 67 as to business at Legislative meetings.

2. Notwithstanding any provision in the Indian Councils Act, 1861, the Governor-General of India in Council may from time to time make rules authorising at any meeting of the Governor-General's Council for the purpose of making laws and regulations the discussion of the annual Financial Statement of the Governor-General in Council and the asking of questions, but under such condition and restrictions as to subject or otherwise as shall be in the said rules prescribed or declared: And notwithstanding any provisions in the Indian Councils Act, 1861, the Governors in Council of Fort St. George and Bombay, respectively, and the Lieutenant-Governor of any province to which the provisions of the Indian Councils Act, 1861, touching the making of laws and regulations, have been more or are hereafter, extended or made applicable, may from time to time make rules for authorising at any meeting of their respective Councils for the purpose of making laws and regulations the discussion of the Annual Financial Statement of their respective local Governments and the asking of questions, but under such conditions and restrictions as to subject or otherwise as shall in the said rules applicable to such Councils respectively be prescribed or declared. But no member at any such meeting of any Council should have power to submit or propose any resolution, or to divide the Council in respect of any such financial discussion, or the answer to any question asked under the authority of this Act, or the rules made under this Act: Provided that any rule made under this Act by a Governor in Council, or by a Lieutenant-Governor, shall be submitted for and shall be subject to the sanction of the Governor-General in Council, and any rule made under this Act by the Governor-General in Council shall be submitted for and shall be subject to the sanction of the Secretary of State in Council: Provided also that rules made under this Act shall not be subject to alteration or amendment at meetings for the purpose of making laws and regulations.

Meaning of 24 & 25 Vict, c. 67, s. 22; 3 & 4 Will. IV, c. 85; & 16 & 17 Vict., c. 95.

3. It is hereby declared that in the twenty-second section of the Indian Councils Act, 1861, it was and is intended that the words "Indian territories now under the dominion of Her Majesty" should be read and construed as if the words "or hereafter" were and had at the time of the passing of the said Act been inserted next after the word "now": and further, that the Acts third and fourth, William the Fourth, Chapter eighty-five, and sixteenth and seventeenth Victoria, Chapter ninety-five respectively, shall be read and construed as if at the date of the enactment thereof respectively it was intended and had been enacted that the said Acts respectively should extend to and include the territories acquired after the dates thereof respectively by the East India

Company, and should not be confined to the territories at the dates of the said enactments respectively in the possession and under the Government of the said Company.

4. Sections thirteen and thirty-two of the Indian Councils Act, 1861, are hereby repealed, and it is enacted that— *Repeal. Power to fill up vacancy in number of additional members.*

(1) If any additional member of Council or any members of the Council of a Lieutenant-Governor appointed under the said Act or this Act shall be absent from India or unable to attend to the duties of his office for a period of two consecutive months, it shall be lawful for the Governor-General, the Governor, or the Lieutenant-Governor to whose Council such additional member or member may have been nominated (as the case may be) to declare, by a notification published in the Government *Gazette*, that the seat in Council of such person has become vacant.

(2) In the event of a vacancy occurring by the absence from India, inability to attend to duty, death, acceptance of office, or resignation duly accepted of any such additional member or member of the Council of a Lieutenant-Governor, or it shall be lawful for the Governor-General, for the Governor, or for the Lieutenant-Governor, as the case may be, to nominate any person as additional member or member, as the case may be, in his place; and every member so nominated shall be summoned to all meetings held for the purpose of making laws and regulations for the term of two years from the date of such nomination: Provided always that it shall not be lawful by such nomination, or by any other nomination made under this Act, to diminish the proportion of non-official members directed by the Indian Councils Act, 1861, to be nominated.

5. The local legislature of any province in India may from time to time, by Acts passed under and subject to the provisions of the Indian Councils Act, 1861, and with the previous sanction of the Governor-General but not otherwise, repeal or amend as to that province any law or regulation made either before or after the passing of this Act by any authority in India other than that local legislature: Provided that an Act or a provision of an Act made by a local legislature, and subsequently assented to by the Governor-General in pursuance of the Indian Councils Act, 1861, shall not be deemed invalid by reason only of its requiring the previous sanction of the Governor-General under this section. *Powers of Indian provincial legislatures.*

Definitions. 6. In this Act—

The expression "local legislature" means—

(1) The Governor in Council for the purpose of making laws and regulations of the respective provinces of Fort St. George and Bombay; and

(2) The Council for the purpose of making laws and regulations of the Lieutenant Governor of any province to which the provisions of the Indian Councils Act, 1861, touching the making of laws or regulations have been or are hereafter extended or made applicable.

The expression "Province" means any presidency, division, province or territory over which the powers of any local legislature for the time being extend.

Saving power of Governor-General in Council.

7. Nothing in this Act shall detract from or diminish the powers of the Governor-General in Council at meetings for the purpose of making laws and regulations.

Short title.

8. This Act may be cited as the Indian Councils Act, 1892; and the Indian Councils Act, 1861, and this Act may be cited together as the Indian Councils Acts, 1861 and 1892.

THE INDIAN COUNCILS ACT (1861.)

An Act to make better Provision for the Constitution of the Council of the Governor-General of India, and for the Local Government of the several Presidencies and Provinces of India, and for the temporary Government of India in the event of a Vacancy in the Office of Governor-General.

[*1st August 1861.*]

WHEREAS it is expedient that the provisions of former Acts of Parliament respecting the constitution and functions of the Council of the Governor-General of India should be consolidated and in certain respects amended, and that power should be given to the Governors in Council of the Presidencies of Fort Saint George and Bombay to make laws and regulations for the government of the said Presidencies; and that provision should be made for constituting the like authority in other parts of Her Majesty's Indian dominions: Be it therefore declared and enacted by the Queen's most excellent Majesty, by and with the advice and consent of the lords spiritual and temporal, and commons, in this present Parliament assembled, and by the authority of the same, as follows:

1. This Act may be cited for all purposes as "The Indian Councils Act, 1861. Short title.

2. Sections forty, forty-three, forty four, fifty, sixty-six, Acts and seventy, and so much of sections sixty-one and sixty-four as parts of Acts relates to vacancies in the office of ordinary member of the repealed. Council of India, of the Act of the third and fourth years of King William the Fourth, chapter eighty-five, for effecting an arrangement with the East India Company, and for the better Government of Her Majesty's Indian territories, till the thirtieth day of April, one thousand eight hundred and fifty-four, sections twenty-two, twenty-three, twenty-four, and twenty-six of the Act of the sixteenth and seventeenth years of Her Majesty, chapter ninety-five, "to provide for the Government of India," and the Act of the twenty-third and twenty-fourth years of Her Majesty, chapter eighty-seven, "to remove doubts as to the authority of the senior "member of the Council of the Governor-General of India in the "absence of the president," are hereby repealed; and all other enactments whatsoever now in force with relation to the Council of the Governor-General of India, or to the Councils of the Governors of the respective Presidencies of Fort Saint George and Bombay, shall, save so far as the same are altered by or are

repugnant to this Act, continue in force, and be applicable to the Council of the Governor-General of India and the Councils of the respective Presidencies under this Act.

Composition of the Council of the Governor-General of India.

3. There shall be ordinary members of the said Council of the Governor-General, three of whom shall from time to time be appointed . . . . from among such persons as shall have been, at the time of such appointment, in the service in India of the Crown, or of the Company and the Crown, for at least ten years; and if the person so appointed shall be in the military service of the Crown, he shall not, during his continuance in office as a member of Council, hold any military command, or be employed in actual military duties; and the remaining two, one of whom shall be a barrister or a member of the Faculty of Advocates in Scotland of not less than five years standing, shall be appointed from time to time by Her Majesty by warrant under Her Royal Sign Manual; and it shall be lawful for the Secretary of State in Council to appoint the Commander-in-Chief of Her Majesty's Forces in India to be an extraordinary member of the said Council, and such extraordinary member of Council shall have rank and precedence at the Council Board next after the Governor-General.

Present members of Council to continue. Appointment of fifth member, and salaries of members, &c.

4. The present ordinary members of the Council of the Governor-General of India shall continue to be ordinary members under and for the purposes of this Act; and it shall be lawful for Her Majesty, on the passing of this Act, to appoint by warrant as aforesaid an ordinary member of Council, to complete the number of five hereby established; and there shall be paid to such ordinary member, and to all other ordinary members who may be hereafter appointed, such amount of salary as may from time to time be fixed for members of the Council of the Governor-General by the Secretary of State in Council, with the concurrence of a majority of members of Council present at a meeting; and all enactments of any Act of Parliament or law of India respecting the Council of the Governor-General of India and the members thereof shall be held to apply to the said Council as constituted by this Act, except so far as they are repealed by or are repugnant to any provisions of this Act.

Provisional appointments of members of Council.

5. It shall be lawful for the Secretary of State in Council, with the concurrence of a majority of members present at a meeting, and for Her Majesty, by warrant as aforesaid, respectively, to appoint any person provisionally to succeed to the office of ordinary member of the Council of the Governor-General, when the same shall become vacant by the death or resignation of the person holding the said office, or on his departure from India with intent to return to Europe, or on any event and contingency expressed in any such provisional appointment, and such appointment again to revoke; but no person so appointed to succeed

provisionally to such office shall be entitled to any authority, salary, or emolument appertaining thereto until he shall be in the actual possession of such office.

6. Whenever the said Governor-General in Council shall declare that it is expedient that the said Governor-General should visit any part of India unaccompanied by his Council, it shall be lawful for the said Governor-General in Council, previously to the departure of the Governor-General, to nominate some member of the said Council to be president of the said Council, in whom, during the time of such visit, the powers of the said Governor-General in assemblies of the said Council shall be reposed, except that of assenting to or withholding his assent from, or reserving for the signification of Her Majesty's pleasure, any law or regulation, as herein-after provided; and it shall be lawful in every such case for the said Governor-General in Council, by an order for that purpose to be made, to authorize the Governor-General alone to exercise all or any of the powers which might be exercised by the said Governor-General in Council in every case in which the said Governor-General may think it expedient to exercise the same, except the power of making laws or regulations. *Provisions during absence of Governor-General in other parts of India.*

7. Whenever the Governor-General, or such president so nominated as aforesaid, shall be obliged to absent himself from any meeting of Council (other than meetings for the purpose of making laws and regulations, as herein-after provided,) owing to indisposition or any other cause whatsoever, and shall signify his intended absence to the Council, then and in every such case the senior member for the time being who shall be present at such meeting shall preside thereat, in such manner, and with such full powers and authorities during the time of such meeting, as such Governor-General or president would have had in case he had been present at such meeting; provided always, that no act of Council made at any such meeting shall be valid to any effect whatsoever unless the same shall be signed by such Governor-General or president respectively, if such Governor-General or president shall at the time be resident at the place at which such meeting shall be assembled, and shall not be prevented by such indisposition from signing the same: Provided always, that in case such Governor-General or president, not being so prevented as aforesaid, shall decline or refuse to sign such act of Council, he, and the several members of Council who shall have signed the same, shall mutually exchange with and communicate in writing to each other the grounds and reasons of their respective opinions, in like manner and subject to such regulations and ultimate responsibility as are by an Act of the thirty-third year of King George the Third, chapter fifty-two, sections forty-seven, forty-eight, forty-nine, fifty, and fifty-one, provided and described in cases where such Governor-General shall, when present, dissent from any measure proposed or agitated in the Council. *Provisions in case of absence of Governor-General, &c. from meeting of Council.* 33 Geo. 3. c. 52. ss. 47 to 51.

Power of Governor-General to make rules for conduct of business.	8. It shall be lawful for the Governor-General from time to time to make rules and orders for the more convenient transaction of business in the said Council; and any order made or act done in accordance with such rules and orders (except as hereafter provided respecting laws and regulations) shall be deemed to be the order or act of the Governor-General in Council.
Council, where to assemble.	9. The said Council shall from time to time assemble at such place or places as shall be appointed by the Governor-General in Council within the territories of India; and as often as the said Council shall assemble within either of the Presidencies of Fort Saint George or Bombay, the Governor of such Presidency shall act as an extraordinary member of Council; and as often as the said Council shall assemble within any other division, province, or territory having a Lieutenant-Governor, such Lieutenant-Governor shall act as an additional councillor at meetings of the Council, for the purpose of making laws and regulations only, in manner herein-after provided.
Additional members to be summoned for the purpose of making laws and regulations.	10. For the better exercise of the power of making laws and regulations vested in the Governor-General in Council the Governor-General shall nominate, in addition to the ordinary and extraordinary members above mentioned, and to such Lieutenant-Governor in the case aforesaid, such persons, not less than six nor more than twelve in number, as to him may seem expedient, to be members of Council for the purpose of making laws and regulations only; and such persons shall not be entitled to sit or vote at any meeting of Council, except at meetings held for such purpose: Provided, that not less than one-half of the persons so nominated shall be non-official persons, that is, persons who, at the date of such nomination, shall not be in the civil or military service of the Crown in India; and that the seat in Council of any non-official member accepting office under the Crown in India shall be vacated on such acceptance.
Such member to be appointed for two years.	11. Every additional member of Council so nominated shall be summoned to all meetings held for the purpose of making laws and regulations, for the term of two years from the date of such nomination.
Resignation of additional members.	12. It shall be lawful for any such additional member of Council to resign his office to the Governor-General; and on acceptance of such resignation by the Governor-General such office shall become vacant.
Power to fill up vacancy in number of additional members.	13. On the event of a vacancy occurring by the death, acceptance of office, or resignation, accepted in manner aforesaid, of any such additional member of Council, it shall be lawful for the Governor-General to nominate any person as additional member of Council in his place, who shall exercise the same functions until

the termination of the term for which the additional member so dying, accepting office, or resigning was nominated: Provided always, that it shall not be lawful for him by such nomination to diminish the proportion of non-official additional members hereinbefore directed to be nominated.

14. No law or regulation made by the Governor-General in Council in accordance with the provisions of this Act shall be deemed invalid by reason only that the proportion of non-official additional members hereby provided was not complete at the date of its introduction to the Council or its enactment. *No law to be invalid by reason of number of non-official members being incomplete.*

15. In the absence of the Governor-General and of the president, nominated as aforesaid, the senior ordinary member of the Council present shall preside at meetings of the Council for making laws and regulations; and the power of making laws and regulations vested in the Governor-General in Council shall be exercised only at meetings of the said Council at which such Governor-General or president, or some ordinary member of Council and six or more members of the said Council, (including under the term members of the Council such additional members as aforesaid), shall be present; and in every case of difference of opinion at meetings of the said Council for making laws and regulations, where three shall be an equality of voices, the Governor-General, or in his absence the president, and in the absence of the Governor-General and president such senior ordinary member of Council there presiding, shall have two votes or the casting vote. *Senior ordinary member of Council to preside at meetings for making laws and regulations in absence of Governor-General, &c. Quorum.*

16. The Governor General in Council shall, as soon as conveniently may be, appoint a place and time for the first meeting of the said Council of the Governor-General for making laws and regulations under this Act, and summon thereto as well the additional councillors nominated by and under this Act as the other members of such Council; and until such first meeting the powers now vested in the said Governor-General of India in Council of making laws and regulations shall and may be exercised in like manner and by the same members as before the passing of this Act. *Governor General to appoint first meeting for making laws and regulations.*

17. It shall be lawful for the Governor-General in Council from time to time to appoint all other times and places of meeting of the Council for the purpose of making laws and regulations under the provisions of this Act, and to adjourn, or from time to time to authorize such president, or senior ordinary member of Council in his absence, to adjourn any meeting for the purpose of making laws and regulations from time to time and from place to place. *Power to appoint and adjourn meetings for making laws and regulations.*

18. It shall be lawful for the Governor-General in Council to make rules for the conduct of business at meetings of the *Rules for conduct of*

[10]

<small>business at such meetings.</small> Council for the purpose of making laws and regulations under the provisions of this Act, prior to the first of such meetings; but such rules may be subsequently amended at meetings for the purpose of making laws or regulations, subject to the assent of the Governor-General; and such rules shall prescribe the mode of promulgation and authentication of such laws and regulations: Provided always, that it shall be lawful for the Secretary of State in Council to disallow any such rule, and to render it of no effect.

<small>Business to be transacted at such meetings</small> 19. No business shall be transacted at any meeting for the purpose of making laws and regulations, except as last hereinbefore provided, other than the consideration and enactment of measures introduced in the Council for the purpose of such enactment; and it shall not be lawful for any member or additional member to make or for the Council to entertain any motion, unless such motion be for leave to introduce some measure as aforesaid into Council, or have reference to some measure actually introduced therein; Provided always, that it shall not be lawful for any member or additional member to introduce, without the previous sanction of the Governor-General, any measure affecting,—

    1st. The public debt or public revenues of India, or by which any charge would be imposed on such revenues:
    2nd. The religion or religious rights and usages of any class of Her Majesty's subjects in India.
    3rd. The discipline or maintenance of any part of Her Majesty's Military or Naval Forces:
    4th. The relations of the Government with foreign princes or states.

<small>Assents of Governor-General to laws and regulations made at such meetings.</small> 20. When any law or regulation has been made by the Council at a meeting for the purpose of making laws and regulations as aforesaid, it shall be lawful for the Governor-General, whether he shall or shall not have been present in Council at the making thereof, to declare that he assents to the same, or that he withholds his assent from the same, or that he reserves the same for the signification of the pleasure of Her Majesty thereon; and no such law or regulation shall have validity until the Governor-General shall have declared his assent to the same, or until (in the case of a law or regulation so reserved as aforesaid) Her Majesty shall have signified her assent to the same to the Governor-General, through the Secretary of State for India in Council, and such assent shall have been duly proclaimed by the said Governor-General.

<small>Power of the Crown to disallow laws and regulations made at such meetings.</small> 21. Whenever any such law or regulation has been assented to by the Governor-General, he shall transmit to the Secretary of State for India an authentic copy thereof; and it shall be lawful for Her Majesty to signify, through the Secretary of State for India in Council, her disallowance of such law; and such disallowance shall make void and annul such law from or after the day

on which the Governor-General shall make known, by proclamation or by signification to his Council, that he has received the notification of such disallowance by Her Majesty.

22. The Governor-General in Council shall have power at meetings for the purpose of making laws and regulations as aforesaid, and subject to the provisions herein contained, to make laws and regulations for repealing, amending, or altering any laws or regulations whatever now in force or hereafter to be in force in the Indian territories now under the dominion of Her Majesty, and to make laws and regulations for all persons, whether British or native, foreigners or others, and for all courts of justice whatever, and for all places and things whatever within the said territories, and for all servants of the Government of India within the dominions of princes and states in alliance with Her Majesty*; and the laws and regulations so to be made by the Governor-General in Council shall control and supersede any laws and regulations in anywise repugnant thereto which shall have been made prior thereto by the Governors of the Presidencies of Fort St. George and Bombay respectively in Council, or the Governor or Lieutenant-Governor in Council of any presidency or other territory for which a Council may be appointed, with power to make laws and regulations, under and by virtue of this Act: Provided always, that the said Governor-General in Council shall not have the power of making any laws or regulations which shall repeal or in any way affect any of the provisions of this Act: *Extent of the powers of the Governor-General in Council to make laws and regulations at such meetings.*

> Or any of the provisions of the Acts of the third and fourth years of King William the Fourth, chapter eighty-five, and of the sixteenth and seventeenth years of Her Majesty, chapter ninety-five, and of the seventeenth and eighteenth years of Her Majesty, chapter seventy-seven, which after the passing of this Act shall remain in force:

> Or any provisions of the Act of the twenty-first and twenty-second years of Her Majesty, chapter one hundred and six, entitled "An Act for the better government of India," or of the Act of the twenty-second and twenty-third years of Her Majesty, chapter forty-one, to amend the same:

> Or of any Act enabling the Secretary of State in Council to raise money in the United Kingdom for the Government of India:

> Or of the Acts for punishing mutiny and desertion in Her Majesty's Army or in Her Majesty's Indian Forces respectively; but subject to the provision contained in the Act of the third and fourth years of King William the Fourth, chapter eighty-five, section seventy-three, respecting the Indian articles of war.

---

* See also 28 Vict., c. 17, s. 1, and 32 & 33 Vict., c. 98, s. 1.

Or any provisions of any Act* passed in this present session of Parliament, or hereafter to be passed, in anywise affecting Her Majesty's Indian territories, or the inhabitants thereof:

Or which may affect the authority of Parliament, or the contitution and rights of the East India Company, or any part of the unwritten laws or constitution of the United Kingdom of Great Britain and Ireland, whereon may depend in any degree the allegiance of any person to the Crown of the United Kingdom, or the sovereignty or dominion of the Crown over any part of the said territories.

<small>Governor-General may make ordinances having force of law in case of urgent necessity.</small>

23. Notwithstanding anything in this Act contained, it shall be lawful for the Governor-General, in cases of emergency, to make and promulgate from time to time ordinances for the peace and good government of the said territories or of any part thereof, subject however to the restrictions contained in the last preceding section; and every such ordinance shall have like force of law with a law or regulation made by the Governor-General in Council, as by this Act provided, for the space of not more than six months from its promulgation, unless the disallowance of such ordinance by Her Majesty shall be earlier signified to the Governor-General by the Secretary of State for India in Council, or unless such ordinance shall be controlled or superseded by some law or regulation made by the Governor-General in Council at a meeting for the purpose of making laws and regulations as by this Act provided.

<small>No law, &c. invalid by reason of its affecting the prerogative of the Crown.</small>

24. No law or regulation made by the Governor-General in Council (subject to the power of disallowance by the Crown, as herein-before provided,) shall be deemed invalid by reason only that it affects the prerogative of the Crown.

25. Whereas doubts have been entertained whether the Governor-General of India, or the Governor-General of India in Council, had the power of making rules, laws, and regulations for the territories known from time to time as "Non-Regulation Provinces," except at meetings for making laws and regulations in conformity with the provisions of the said Acts of the third and fourth years of King William the Fourth, chapter eighty-five, and of the sixteenth and seventeenth years of Her Majesty, chapter ninety-five, and whether the Governor, or Governor in Council, or Lieutenant-Governor of any presidency or part of India, had such power in respect of any such territories: Be it enacted, that no rule, law, or regulation which prior to the passing of this Act shall have been made by the Governor-General, or Governor-General in Council, or by any other of the

<small>Laws made for the non-regulation provinces declared valid.</small>

---

* *Queen* v. *Msares* 14 Beng. 106, 112.

authorities aforesaid, for and in respect of any such non-regulation province, shall be deemed invalid only by reason of the same not having been made in conformity with the provisions of the said Acts, or of any other Act of Parliament respecting the constitution and powers of the Council of India or of the Governor-General, or respecting the powers of such Governors, or Governors in Council, or Lieutenant-Governors as aforesaid.

26. It shall be lawful for the Governor-General in Council, or Governor in Council of either of the Presidencies, as the case may be, to grant to an ordinary member of Council leave of absence, under medical certificate, for a period not exceeding six months; and such member, during his absence, shall retain his office, and shall, on his return and resumption of his duties, receive half his salary* for the period of such absence; but if his absence shall exceed six months, his office shall be vacated. *Provision for leave of absence to an ordinary member of Council.*

27. If any vacancy shall happen in the office of an ordinary member of the Council of the Governor-General, or of the Council of either of the Presidencies, when no person provisionally appointed to succeed thereto shall be then present on the spot, then, and on every such occasion, such vacancy shall be supplied by the appointment of the Governor-General in Council, or the Governor in Council as the case may be; and until a successor shall arrive the person so nominated shall execute the office to which he shall have been appointed, and shall have all the powers thereof, and shall have and be entitled to the salary and other emoluments and advantages appertaining to the said office during his continuance therein, every such temporary member of Council foregoing all salaries and allowances by him held and enjoyed at the time of his being appointed to such office; and if any ordinary member of the Council of the Governor-General, or of the Council of either of the Presidencies, shall, by any infirmity or otherwise, be rendered incapable of acting or of attending to act as such, or if any such member shall be absent on leave, and if any person shall have been provisionally appointed as aforesaid, then the place of such member absent or unable to attend shall be supplied by such person; and if no person provisionally appointed to succeed to the office shall be then on the spot, the Governor-General in Council, or Governor in Council, as the case may be, shall appoint some person to be a temporary member of Council; and, until the return of the member so absent or unable to attend, the person so provisionally appointed by the Secretary of State in Council, or so appointed by the Governor-General in Council, or Governor in Council as the case may be, shall execute the office to which he shall have been appointed, and shall have all the powers thereof, and shall receive half the salary of the member of Council *Power of making temporary appointments of members of Council, &c.*

---

* See 3 & 4 Wm. IV, c. 85, s. 77, *supra*, p, 239.

[14]

whose place he supplies, and also half the salary of his office under the Government of India, or the Government of either of the Presidencies, as the case may be, if he hold any such office, the remaining half of such last-named salary being at the disposal of the Government of India, or other Government as aforesaid: Provided always, that no person shall be appointed a temporary member of the said Council who might not have been appointed as hereinbefore provided to fill the vacancy supplied by such temporary appointment.

Governors of Fort Saint George and Bombay may make rules for the conduct of business in their Councils.

28. It shall be lawful for the Governors of the Presidencies of Fort Saint George and Bombay, respectively, from time to time to make rules and orders for the conduct of business in their Councils, and any order made or act done in accordance with such directions (except as herein-after provided respecting laws and regulations) shall be deemed to be the order or act of the Governor in Council.

Power to summon additional members to the Councils of Fort Saint George and Bombay for the purposes of making laws and regulations.

29. For the better exercise of the power of making laws and regulations herein-after vested in the Governors of the said Presidencies in Council respectively, each of the said Governors shall, in addition to the members whereof his Council now by law consists, or may consist, termed herein ordinary members, nominate to be additional members the Advocate-General of the Presidency, or officer acting in that capacity, and such other persons, not less than four nor more than eight in number, as to him may seem expedient, to be members of Council, for the purpose of making laws and regulations only; and such members shall not be entitled to sit or vote at any meeting of Council, except at meetings held for such purpose; provided, that not less than half of the persons so nominated shall be non-official persons, as hereinbefore described; and that the seat in Council of any non-official member accepting office under the Crown in India shall be vacated on such acceptance.

Such members to be appointed for two years.

30. Every additional member of Council so nominated shall be summoned to all meetings held for the purpose of making laws and regulations for the term of two years the date of such nomination.

Resignation of additional members.

31. It shall be lawful for any such additional member of Council to resign his office to the Governor of the Presidency; and on acceptance of such resignation by the Governor of the Presidency such office shall become vacant.

Power to fill up vacancy in the number of additional members.

32. On the event of a vacancy occurring by the death, acceptance of office, or resignation accepted in manner aforesaid, of any such additional member of Council, it shall be lawful for the Governor of the Presidency to summon any person as additional member of Council in his place, who shall exercise the same

[15]

functions until the termination of the term for which the additional member so dying, accepting office, or resigning, was nominated : Provided always, it shall not be lawful for him by such nomination to diminish the proportion of non-official members herein-before directed to be nominated.

33. No law or regulation made by any such Governor in Council in accordance with the provisions of this Act shall be deemed invalid by reason only that the proportion of non-official additional members hereby established was not complete at the date of its introduction to the Council or its enactment. *No law to be invalid by reason of incompleteness of number of non-official members.*

34. At any meeting of the Council of either of the said Presidencies from which the Governor shall be absent, the senior civil ordinary member of Council present shall preside; and the power of making laws and regulations hereby vested in such Governor in Council shall be exercised only at meetings of such Council at which the Governor or some ordinary member of Council, and four or more members of Council (including under the term members of Council such additional members as aforesaid), shall be present; and in any case of difference of opinion at meetings of any such Council for making laws and regulations, where there shall be an equality of voices, the Governor, or in his absence the senior member then presiding, shall have two votes or the casting vote. *Senior civil ordinary member of Council to preside in absence of Governor of Presidency.*

35. The Governor-General in Council shall, as soon as conveniently may be, appoint the time for the first meeting of the Councils of Fort Saint George and Bombay respectively, for the purpose of making laws and regulations under this Act; and the Governors of the said Presidencies respectively shall summon to such meeting as well the additional Councillors appointed by and under this Act as the ordinary members of the said Councils. *Governor-General to fix first meeting of Councils of Presidencies for making laws and regulations, &c.*

36. It shall be lawful for every such Governor to appoint all subsequent times and places of meeting of his Council for the purpose of making laws and regulations under the provisions of this Act, and to adjourn or from time to time to authorize such senior ordinary member of Council in his absence to adjourn any meeting for making laws and regulations from time to time and from place to place. *Governors of Presidencies to appoint subsequent meetings, and adjourn them.*

37. Previously to the first of such meetings of their Councils for the purpose of making laws and regulations under the provisions of this Act, the Governors of the said Presidencies in Council respectively shall make rules for the conduct of business at such meetings, subject to the sanction of the Governor-General in Council; but such rules may be subsequently amended at meetings for the purpose of making laws and regulations, subject to the assent of the Governor : Provided always, that it shall be *Rules for conduct of business at such meetings.*

lawful for the Governor-General in Council to disallow any such rule, and render the same of no effect.

Business to be transacted at such meetings. 38. No business shall be transacted at any meeting of the Council of either of the said Presidencies for the purpose of making laws and regulations (except as last herein-before provided) other than the consideration and enactment of measures introduced into such Council for the purpose of such enactment; and it shall not be lawful for any member or additional member to make, or for the Council to entertain, any motion, unless such motion shall be for leave to introduce some measure as aforsaid into Council, or have reference to some measure actually introduced thereinto; Provided always, that it shall not be lawful for any member or additional member to introduce, without the previous sanction of the Governor, any measure affecting the public revenues of the Presidency, or by which any charge shall be imposed on such revenues.

Governors to assent to laws and regulations of Presidencies. 39. When any law or regulation has been made by any such Council at a meeting for the purpose of making laws and regulations as aforesaid, it shall be lawful for the Governor, whether he shall or shall not have been present in Council at such meeting, to declare that he assents to, or withholds his assent from the same.

Governor-General to assent to laws and regulations of Presidencies. 40. The Governor shall transmit forthwith an authentic copy of every law or regulation to which he shall have so declared his assent to the Governor-General; and no such law or regulation shall have validity until the Governor-General shall have assented thereto, and such assent shall have been signified by him to and published by the Governor: Provided always, that in every case where the Governor-General shall withhold his assent from any such law or regulation, he shall signify to the Governor in writing his reason for so withholding his assent.

Power of the Crown to disallow laws and regulations of Presidencies. 41. Whenever any such law or regulation shall have been assented to by the Governor-General, he shall transmit to the Secretary of State for India an authentic copy thereof; and it shall be lawful for Her Majesty to signify, through the Secretary of State for India in Council, her disallowance of such law or regulation; and such disallowance shall make void and annul such law or regulation from or after the day on which such Governor shall make known by proclamation, or by signification to the Council that he has received the notification of such disallowance by Her Majesty.

Extent of power of Governor of Presidency in Council to make laws. 42. The Governor of each of the said Presidencies in Council shall have power, at meetings for the purpose of making laws and regulations as aforesaid, and subject to the provisions herein contained, to make laws and regulations for the peace and good government of such Presidency, and for that purpose to repeal and amend any laws and regulations made prior to the coming into operation of this Act by any authority in India, so far as they affect such Presidency : Provided always, that such Governor in Council shall not have the power of making any laws or regulations which shall in any way affect any of the provisions of this Act, or of any other Act of Parliament in force or hereafter to be in force in such Presidency. and regulations.

43. It shall not be lawful for the Governor in Council of either of the aforesaid Presidencies, except with the sanction of the Governor General, previously communicated to him, to make regulations or take into consideration any law or regulation for any of the purposes next herein-after mentioned ; that is to say, Governor of Presidency, except with sanction of Governor-General, not to make or take into consideration laws and regulations for certain purposes.

1. Affecting the public debt of India, or the customs duties, or any other tax or duty now in force and imposed by the authority of the Government of India for the general purposes of such Government ;
2. Regulating any of the current coin, or the issue of any bills, notes, or other paper currency :
3. Regulating the conveyance of letters by the post office or messages by the electric telegraph within the Presidency :
4. Altering in any way the Penal Code of India, as established by Act of the Governor General in Council, No. 42* of 1860 :
5. Affecting the religion or religious rites and usages of any class of Her Majesty's subjects in India :
6. Affecting the discipline or maintenance of any part of Her Majesty's Military or Naval Forces :
7. Regulating patents or copyright :
8. Affecting the relations of the Government with foreign princes or states :

Provided always, that no law or provision of any law or regulation which shall have been made by any such Governor in Council, and assented to by the Governor General as aforesaid, shall be deemed invalid only by reason of its relating to any of the purposes comprised in the above list.

44. The Governor General in Council, so soon as it shall appear to him expedient, shall, by proclamation, extend the provisions of this Act touching the making of laws and regulations for the peace and good government of the Presidencies of Fort Saint George and Bombay to the Bengal division of the Presidency of Fort William, and shall specify in such proclamation the period Governer-General may establish Councils for making laws and regulations in the

---

* Should be " No. 45."

3

[18]

<small>Presidency of Fort William in Bengal, &c.</small> at which such provisions shall take effect,* and the number of councillors whom the Lieutenant Governor of the said division may nominate for his assistance in making laws and regulations ; and it shall be further lawful for the Governor General in Council, from time to time and in his discretion, by similar proclamation, to extend the same provisions to the territories known as the North-Western Provinces and the Punjab respectively.

<small>Constitution of such Councils.</small> 45. Whenever such proclamation as aforesaid shall have been issued regarding the said division or territories respectively, the Lieutenant Governor thereof shall nominate, for his assistance in making laws and regulations, such number of councillors as shall be in such proclamation specified ; provided, that not less than one-third of such councillors shall in every case be non-official persons, as herein-before described, and that the nomination of such councillors shall be subject to the sanction of the Governor General ; and provided further, that at any meeting of any such Council from which the Lieutenant Governor shall be absent, the member highest in official rank among those who may hold office under the Crown shall preside ; and the power of making laws and regulations shall be exercised only at meetings at which the Lieutenant Governor, or some member holding office as aforesaid, and not less than one-half of the members of Council so summoned as aforesaid, shall be present ; and in any case of difference of opinion at any meetings of such Council for making laws and regulations, where there shall be an equality of voices, the Lieutenant Governor, or such member highest in official rank as aforesaid then presiding, shall have two votes or the casting vote.

<small>Power to constitute new provinces, and appoint Lieutenant-Governors.</small> 46. It shall be lawful for the Governor General, by proclamation as aforesaid, to constitute from time to time new provinces for the purposes of this Act, to which the like provisions shall be applicable ; and further to appoint from time to time a Lieutenant Governor to any province so constituted as aforesaid, and from time to time to declare and limit the extent of the authority of such Lieutenant Governor, inlikemanner as is provided by the Act of the seventeenth and eighteenth years of Her Majesty, chapter seventy-seven, respecting the Lieutenant Governors of Bengal and the North-western Provinces.

<small>Power to alter boundaries of presidencies, &c. by proclamation.</small> 47. It shall be lawful for the Governor General in Council, by such proclamation as aforesaid, to fix the limits of any presidency, division, province, or territory in India for the purpose of this Act, and further by proclamation to divide or alter from time to time the limits of any such presidency, division, province, or territory for the said purposes : Provided always, that any law or regulation made by the Governor or Lieutenant-Governor in

---

* 28th January, 1892, see *Calcutta Gazette*, 1862, pp. 257, 228.

Council of any presidency, division, province, or territory shall continue in force in any part thereof which may be severed therefrom by any such proclamation, until superseded by law or regulation of the Governor General in Council, or of the Governor or Lieutenant Governor in Council of the presidency, division, province, or territory, to which such parts may become annexed.

48. It shall be lawful for every such Lieutenant Governor in Council thus constituted to make laws for the peace and good government of his respective division, province, or territory, and, except as otherwise herein-before specially provided, all the provisions in this Act contained respecting the nomination of additional members for the purpose of making laws and regulations for the Presidencies of Fort Saint George and Bombay, and limiting the power of the Governors in Council of Fort Saint George and Bombay for purpose of making laws and regulations, and respecting the conduct of business in the meetings of such Councils for that purpose, and respecting the power of the Governor General to declare or withhold his assent to laws or regulations made by the Governor in Council of Fort Saint George and Bombay, and respecting the power of Her Majesty to disallow the same, shall apply to laws or regulations to be so made by any such Lieutenant-Governor in Council. *Powers of newly constituted Lieutenant-Governors in Council.*

49. Provided always, that no proclamation to be made by the Governor General in Council under the provisions of this Act for the purpose of constituting any Council for the presidency, division, provinces, or territories herein-before named, or any other provinces, or for altering the boundaries of any presidency, division, province, or territory, or constituting any new province for the purpose of this Act, shall have any force or validity until the sanction of Her Majesty to the same shall have been previously signified by the Secretary of State in Council to the Governor General. *Previous assent of the Crown necessary to give validity to proclamation.*

50. If any vacancy shall happen in the office of Governor General of India when no provisional successor shall be supply such vacancy, then and in every such case the Governor of the Presidency of Fort Saint George or the Governor of the Presidency of Bombay who shall have been first appointed to the office of Governor by Her Majesty, shall hold and execute the said office of Governor General of India and Governor of the Presidency of Fort William in Bengal until a successor shall arrive, or until some person in India shall be duly appointed thereto ; and every such acting Governor General shall, during the time of his continuing to act as such, have and exercise all the rights and powers of Governor General of India, and shall be entitled to receive the emoluments and advantages appertaining to the office by him supplied, such acting Governor-General foregoing the salary and *Provision for India to the supply of the office of Governor-General in certain circumstances.*

allowances appertaining to the office of Governor to which he stands appointed; and such office of Governor shall be supplied for the time during which such Governor shall be supplied for the time which such Governor shall act as Governor General, in the manner directed in section sixty-three of the Act of the third and fourth years of King William the Fourth, chapter eighty-five.

<small>If it appears to the Governor necessary to exercise powers before taking his seat in Council, he may make his appointment, &c. known by proclamation.</small> 51. If, on such vacancy occuring, it shall appear to the Governor, who by virtue of this Act shall hold and execute the said office of Governor General, necessary to exercise the powers thereof before he shall have taken his seat in Council, it shall be lawful for him to make known by proclamation his appointment and his intention to assume the said office of Governor General; and after such proclamation, and thenceforth until he shall repair to the place where the Council may assemble, it shall be lawful for him to exercise alone all or any of the powers which might be exercised by the Governor General in Council, except the power of making laws and regulations; and all acts done in the exercise of the said powers, except as aforesaid, shall be of the same force and effect as if they had been done by the Governor General in Council; provided, that all acts done in the said Council after the date of such proclamation, but before the communication thereof to such Council, shall be valid, subject nevertheless to revocation or alteration by such Governor who shall have so assumed the said office of Governor General; and from the date of the vacancy occurring, until such Governor shall have assumed the said office of Governor General, the provisions of section sixty-two of the Act of the third and fourth years of King William the Fourth, chapter eighty-five, shall be and the same are declared to be applicable to the case.

<small>Nothing in this Act shall derogate from the powers of the Crown of Secretary of State for India in Council.</small> 52. Nothing in this Act contained shall be held to derogate from or interfere with (except as herein-before expressly provided) the rights vested in Her Majesty, or the powers of the Secretary of State for India in Council, in relation to the government of Her Majesty's dominions in India, under any law in force at the date of the passing of this Act; and all things which shall be done by Her Majesty, or by the Secretary of State as aforesaid, in relation to such government, shall have the same force and validity as if this Act had not been passed.

<small>Meaning of term "in Council."</small> 53. Wherever any act or thing is by this Act required or authorized to be done by the Governor General or by the Governors of the Presidencies of Fort Saint George and Bombay in Council, it is not required that such act or thing should be done at a meeting for making laws and regulations, unless where expressly provided.

[20a]

32 & 33 VICTORIA, CHAPTER 98.

An Act to define the powers of the Governor-General of India in Council at meetings for making laws and regulations for certain purposes. [11th August, 1869.]

WHEREAS doubts have arisen as to the extent of power of the Governor-General of India in Council to make laws binding upon native Indian subjects beyond the Indian territories under the dominion of Her Majesty:

And whereas it is expedient that better provision should be made in other respects for the exercise of the power of the Governor-General in Council:

Be it enacted by the Queen's Most Excellent Majesty, by and with the advice and consent of the Lords Spiritual and Temporal, and Commons, in this present Parliament assembled, and by the authority of the same, as follows:—

1. From and after the passing of this Act, the Governor-General of India in Council shall have power at meetings for the purpose of making laws and regulations to make laws and regulations for all persons being native Indian subjects of Her Majesty, Her heirs and successors, without and beyond as well as within the Indian territories under the dominion of Her Majesty.

Power to make laws for native Indian subjects beyond the Indian territories.

2. No law heretofore passed by the Governor-General of India, or by the Governors of Madras and Bombay, respectively in Council, shall be deemed to be invalid solely by reason of its having reference to native subjects of Her Majesty not within the Indian territories under the dominion of Her Majesty.

Former laws to be valid.

3. Notwithstanding anything in the Indian Councils Act or in any other Act of Parliament contained, any law or regulation which shall hereafter be made by the Governor-General in Council in manner in the said Indian Councils Act provided shall not be invalid by reason only that it may repeal or affect any of the provisions of the said Act of the third and fourth years of King William the Fourth, chapter eighty-five, contained in sections eighty-one, eighty-two, eighty-three, eighty-four, eighty-five and eighty-six of the said Act.

Power to repeal or amend certain sections of 3 and 4 W. 4., c. 85.

33 VICTORIA, CHAPTER 3.

An Act to make better provision for making laws and regulations for certain parts of India, and for certain other purposes relating thereto. [25th March 1870.]

WHEREAS it is expedient that provision should be made to enable Governor-General of India in Council to make regulations for the peace and good government of certain territories in India, otherwise than at meetings for the purpose of making laws and regulations held under the provisions of the Indian Councils Act, 1861, and also for certain other purposes connected with the Government of India:

Be it enacted by the Queen's Most Excellent Majesty, by and with the advice and consent of the Lords Spiritual and Temporal, and Commons, in this present Parliament assembled, and by the authority of the same, as follows :—

1. *Power to Executive Government of British India to make regulations for certain parts thereof.* Every Governor of a Presidency in Council, Lieutenant-Governor, or Chief Commissioner, whether the Governorship, or Lieutenant-Governorship, or Chief Commissionership be now in existence or may hereafter be established, shall have power to propose to the Governor-General in Council drafts of any regulations, together with the reasons for proposing the same, for the peace and government of any part or parts of the territories under his Government or Administration to which the Secretary of State for India shall from time to time by resolution in Council declare the provisions of this section to be applicable from any date to be fixed in such resolution.

And the Governor-General in Council shall take such drafts and reasons into consideration; and when any such draft shall have been approved of by the Governor-General in Council, and shall have received the Governor-General's assent, it shall be published in the *Gazette of India* and in the local Gazette, and shall thereupon have like force of law and be subject to the like disallowances as if it had been made by the Governor-General of India in Council at a meeting for the purpose of making laws and regulations.

The Secretary of State for India in Council may from time to time withdraw such power from any Governor, Lieutenant-Governor or Chief Commissioner, on whom it has been conferred, and may from time to time restore the same as he shall think fit.

2. *Copies of regulations to be sent to Secretary of State. Subsequent enactments to control regulations.* The Governor-General shall transmit to the Secretary of State for India in Council an authentic copy of every regulation which shall have been made under the provisions of this Act; and all laws or regulations hereafter made by the Governor-General of India in Coun-

cil, whether at a meeting for the purpose of making laws and regulations, or under the said provisions, shall control and supersede any regulation in anywise repugnant thereto which shall have been made under the same provisions.

<small>Lieutenant-Governors and Chief Commissioners to be members *ex-officio* of the Governor General's Council for the purpose of making laws and regulations.</small>

3. Whenever the Governor-General in Council shall hold a meeting for the purpose of making laws and regulations at any place within the limits of any territories now or hereafter placed under the administration of a Lieutenant-Governor or a Chief Commissioner, the Lieutenant-Governor or Chief Commissioner respectively shall be *ex-officio* and Additional Member of the Council of the Governor-General for that purpose, in excess (if necessary) of the maximum number of twelve spcified by the said Act.

<small>Section 49, of 3 and 4 W. 4, c. 85 repealed.</small>

4. Section forty-nine of the Act of the third and fourth years of King William the Fourth, chapter eighty-five, is hereby repealed.

<small>Procedure in case of difference between the Governor-General and the majority of his Council.</small>

5. Whenever any measure shall be proposed before the Governor-General of India in Council whereby the safety, tranquillity, or interests of the British possessions in India, or any part thereof, are or may be, in the judgment of the said Governor General essentially affected, and he shall be of opinion either that the measure proposed ought to be adopted and carried into execution, or that it ought to be suspended or rejected, and the Majority in Council then present shall dissent from such opinion, the Governor-General may on his own authority and responsibility, suspend or reject the measure in part or in whole, or adopt and carry it into execution, but in every such case any two members of the dissentient majority may require that the said suspension, rejection, or adoption, as well as the fact of their dissent, shall be notified to the Secretary of State for India, and such notification shall be accompanied by copies of the minutes (if any) which the Members of the Council shall have recorded on the subject.

<small>Power to appoint natives of India to certain offices without certificate from the Civil Service Commissioners.</small>

6. Whereas it is expedient that additional facilities should be given for the employment of natives of India, of proved merit and ability, in the Civil Service of Her Majesty in India : Be it enacted, that nothing in the "Act for the Government of India," twenty-one and twenty-two Victoria, chapter one hundred and six, or in the "Act to confirm certain appointments in India, and to amend the law concerning the Civil Service there," twenty-four and twenty-five Victoria, chapter fifty-four, or in any

other Act of Parliament or other law now in force in India, shall restrain the authorities in India by whom appointments are or may be made to offices, places, and employments in the Civil Service of Her Majesty in India from appointing any native of India to any such office, place, or employment, although such native shall not have been admitted to the said Civil Service of India in manner in section thirty-two of the first-mentioned Act provided but subject to such rules as may be from time to time prescribed by the Governor-General in Council, and sanctioned by the Secretary of State in Council, with the concurrence of a majority of members present ; and that for the purpose of this Act the words " natives of India " shall include any person born and domiciled within the dominions of Her Majesty in India, of parents habitually resident in India, and not established there for temporary purposes only ; and that it shall be lawful for the Governor-General in Council to define and limit from time to time the qualification of native of India thus expressed ; provided that every resolution made by him for such purpose shall be subject to the sanction of the Secretary of State in Council, and shall not have force until it has been laid for thirty days before both Houses of Parliament.

34 & 35 VICTORIA, CHAPTER 34.

An Act to extend in certain respects the power of Local Legislatures in India as regards European British subjects.

[29th June 1871.]

WHEREAS it is expedient that the power of making laws and regulations conferred on Governors of Presidencies in India in Council by the Indian Councils Act, 24 & 25 Vict., c. 67, sec. 42, should in certain respects be extended :

Be it enacted by the Queen's Most Excellent Majesty, by and with the advice and consent of the Lords Spiritual and Temporal, and Commons, in this present Parliament assembled, and by the authority of the same, as follows :—

1. No law or regulation heretofore made or hereafter to be made by any Governor or Lieutenant-Governor in Council in India in manner prescribed by the aforesaid Act shall be invalid only by reason that it confers on magistrates, being justices of the peace, the same jurisdiction over European British subjects as such Governor or Lieutenant-Governor in Council, by regulations made as aforesaid, could have lawfully conferred or could lawfully confer on magistrates in the exercise of authority over natives in the like cases.

Power to Local Legislatures to confer jurisdiction over European British subjects to magistrates in certain cases.

2. When evidence has been given in any proceeding under this Act before a magistrate, being a justice of the peace, which appears to be sufficient for the conviction of the accused person, being an European British subject, of an offence for which, if a native, he would under existing law be triable exclusively before the Court of Sessions, or which, in the opinion of the magistrate, is one which ought to be tried by the High Court, the accused person, if such European British subject, shall be sent for trial by the magistrate before the High Court.

Commital of defendant (being an European British subject) to the High Court. (Indian Act No. XXV of 1861, s. 226.)

3. And whereas by an Act passed by the Governor-General of India in Council, Indian Act No. XXII of 1870, it is provided that certain Acts heretofore passed by the Governors of Madras and Bombay respectively in Council, and by the Lieutenant-Governor of Bengal in Council, shall, so far as regards the liability of European British subjects to be convicted and punished thereunder, be and be deemed to be as valid as if they had been passed by the Governor-General of India in Council at a meeting for the purpose of making laws and regulations: Be it further enacted, that the said Governors and Lieutenant-Governor in Council respectively shall have power to repeal and amend any of the said Act so declared valid, by Acts to be passed under the provisions of the Indian Councils Act.

Power to local Legislatures to amend and repeal certain laws.

Memorandum by the British Committee of the Indian National Congress:

THE INDIAN COUNCILS BILL.

(June 1892.)

THE India Councils Bill has now become law, and the conditions under which its most important provision is to be carried out have been left to the discretion of the authorities in India itself. That provision refers to the extension of the Councils taken in connection with the "Northbrook Clause," which permits such extension to be carried out under definite regulations to be framed by the Viceroy. The venue of the controversy has thus for the time been transferred to India, and it becomes the function of the public in each Presidency and Province to place its views before the Viceroy through its local government, and endeavour to obtain a full and real measure of representation. In this connection it is of the first importance to note that the House of Commons not only does not contemplate any limitation of the discretion of the Indian authorities, but anticipates that their discretion will be used in a spirit of genuine liberality. These views are not embodied in the Bill, *literatim et verbatim*, but must be gathered from the speeches of representative men of both parties in the debates in both Houses. The more important of these declarations are collected in the following *catena* of extracts, which at once exhibits the history of the growth of the doctrine of "election or selection," and demonstrates the clearness with which it was finally enunciated.

The "Councils in India Bill" was introduced and read a first time in the House of Lords on the 21st February, 1890. The Bill came up for second reading on March 6th, when the question as to the mode in which the "additional" members should be appointed was first mooted. On that occasion the Earl of Northbrook said:—

"There have of late been proposals made to widen the area of the Legislative Council—I mean by that to increase considerably the numbers of the non-official members; and it has also been suggested that *some sytsem of election or selection*, other than that of simple nomination, should be applied to the choice of the non-official members. . . . . I regret very much that the Government has not been enabled to introduce into this Bill any system whatever by which a portion of the non-official members of the Local Legislatures, at any rate, could be chosen by some system of election or selection, and not left entirely to a system of pure nomination. . . . . I venture to express the hope that it may not be impossible for Her Majesty's Government to reconsider that portion of the Bill, and that they may think it would not be right to shut the door, as would be done by this Bill, to the introduction of some system of selection or election into the subordinate Legislative Councils, at any rate. I have no hesitation in saying that, with proper safeguards, some system of selection of that kind might be safely carried out. . . . . I myself would suggest that it might be possible to introduce a clause into the Bill enabling the Viceroy in Council in India to submit some scheme for the election of part or the whole of the non-official members of the Local Legislatures, for the consideration of the Secretary of State for India in Council, and after the approval of the Secretary of State for India in Council was given it might be carried into effect by proclamation."

Following him the Marquis of Ripon said :—

"With respect to the mode in which any extension of members in the Governor-General's Council or in the Local Councils should be carried out, I agree very much with what fell from my noble friend the Earl of Northbrook, and I earnestly hope Her Majesty's Government will give great weight to what he has said and to the appeal which he has made to them to reconsider the frame of this clause so as to render it possible for the Government of India to introduce into the Local Governments especially, and I would go to the extent of saying the Governor-General's Council also, *the principle of election or selection*, whichever you may call it. Your lordships may remember that, if some such power is not given in this Bill, it will require a fresh Act of Parliament before any change of that kind can be introduced into even the Local Councils. . . . . Therefore I go quite along with my noble friend in saying that you should make such a Bill as this an empowering Bill; that you should lay down the principle on which these Councils are to be constituted, but that you should leave the details as much as you can to be arranged by the Government and Legislatures of India."

The demand thus clearly and unequivocally made was supported by the Earl of Kimberley and Lord Stanley of Alderley. The opposite contention of the Government was maintained by Lords Salisbury and Cross. Both speeches were, in form at least, opposed to the popular request, and need not therefore be quoted here; but there was one striking difference between them, a difference which was pointed out at the moment by the late Earl Granville. He said :—

"My lords, it is impossible not to remark upon how very much more strongly the noble Marquess has met the objections which have been stated upon this side of the House than has been done by the noble Secretary of State for the India Department. Really, the speech of the noble Marquis (Salisbury) puts an absolute stop to any such suggestion as has been made. I think that argument has been put a little too high in this sense : it would be really supposed that the suggestion made by the noble Earl (Northbrook) behind me, and which was supported by the noble Marquis (Ripon) who, of course, was speaking with immense weight and authority upon this particular subject, was, as far as this House is concerned, that the House should amend the Bill and send out a complete cut and dried Parliamentary constitution for India upon this occasion. But against that my noble friend the Earl of Northbrook specially guarded himself, and he pointed out that we were not in a position to judge how anything of this kind was to be carried out, but that it was desirable to give the Viceroy, or the Governor, or Lieutenant-Governor, more power than he now possesses in order to carry out any such matters. It appears to me that the noble Marquis (Ripon) in his speech, has dealt with the matter with great authority and weight."

In fact, while the speech of the Marquis of Salisbury was uncompromising in its hostility, that of Viscount Cross was marked by great generality, and was evidently intended to leave a loophole of escape, if necessary, in the future.

This discussion is of extreme importance in connection with the Committee stage of the Bill; but before passing on to that, attention must be called to a very important passage in the speech of Lord Salisbury, as follows :—

"What appeared to me to be most alarming in the reasoning of the noble lords opposite was that they seemed to think they could stumble and slip into this great change, and that no harm would come to them if they had not taken count beforehand where their steps were to be placed or in what direction their journey was to be taken. *You must not drift* into an elective Government of India. You must make up your mind how you are to frame your constituencies, how those vast interests are to be represented, before you consign yourselves to the charge, and Government of the most powerful principle that affects political communities. Do not imagine that you can introduce it in small doses, and that it will be satisfied by that concession. At least we know this of the elective principle from our experience in Europe, that wherever it has made for itself a small channel it has been able to widen and widen that channel gradually until all has been carried before it, and that is the danger of any action you may take in India. I hope we shall not imagine that when once we have consigned ourselves to this principle, we can retrace out steps or take away the powers that we have given, or that we can undo the result of any mistake we may make. I, therefore, earnestly urge upon the House not to make so great a change without the most careful and circumspect examination of all the difficulties and dangers which surround it; not to slip into this great innovation as it were accidentally. But if we are to do it, if it has to be done, let us do it systematically, counting the cost, examining all the details, and *taking care that the machinery to be provided shall effect the purpose of giving representation*, not to accidentally constituted bodies, not to small sections of the people here and there, but *to the living strength and vital forces of the whole community of India*."

Now this warning must be held to be addressed, not only to the noble lords opposite in 1890, but to Liberals and Conservatives, peers and commoners, alike, in 1892, after a period of two years for "careful and circumspect examination". The Government and their supporters in India are now completely estopped from setting up any defence of having stumbled or slipped into any great change, they have walked into it with their eyes open, and with full premeditation. And since they have done so their duty now is to carry out the precept of the Premier, by giving representation to " *the living strength and vital forces of the whole community*."

The House proceeded to consider the Bill in Committee on March 13; when, with the view of making it quite clear that it would be legal for the various heads of Governments to nominate persons recommended to them by various (unspecified) public bodies, the Earl of Northbrook moved to add the following words (since commonly called " the Northbrook Clause") to Clause 1 of the Bill.

" Provided that the Governor-General in Council may from time to time, with the approval of the Secretary of State in Council, make regulations as to the conditions under which such nominations or any of them shall be made by the Governor-General, Governors, and Lieutenant-Governors, respectively, and describe the manner in which such regulations shall be carried into effect."

In accepting this amendment, Viscount Cross said :—

"It had always been my intention when this Bill became law, which I hope will soon be the case, to follow the example of Sir Charles Wood, and in sending out a copy of the Act to send with it a despatch pointing out how these members of Council might very well be nominated so as not only to give the Governor-General, the Governors, and Lieutenant-Governors the sufficient additional assistance which they might require, but so as they might get the best representatives of the people of the country. But the noble lord has said that there might be some possible legal difficulty experienced in carrying that out unless there was something in the Act of Parliament showing how that might be done. Nothing is farther from my mind than to leave a legal difficulty open for further dispute; therefore, I have not the smallest objection to insert such words in order to make quite clear the intention of the Legislature in passing this Act of Parliament. There is one further advantage in inserting words of this kind, that it will satisfy the people of India that this matter has been thought of and considered when they find that this particular matter is referred to in the Act itself, which practically increases the number of persons to be nominated."

And Earl Kimberley followed thus :—

"My lords, I am extremely glad to hear that the noble Viscount will accept the words proposed by the noble lord behind me. I am bound to say that I can express my satisfaction because I regard this as *to a certain extent admitting the elective principle*. I understand that this Bill will enable the Governor-General to put into the hands of certain public bodies the selection of the persons who are to be nominated by him to the Council. That may not be, strictly speaking, what we should call election, but I welcome this clause as opening the door, because I should wish to leave open the door to the Government to practically leave the selection to bodies who will, in fact, elect the representatives."

The Bill was not proceeded with in 1891, but that the Government intended to make a strong feature of it in the last session if the present Parliament became apparent from the debate on the Address. Earl Dudley, in the House of Lords said : " It has been long and carefully considered by the Indian Government, who are most anxious that Her Majesty's Indian subjects should have this gradual and judicious extension of responsibility."

In the Commons it was alluded to by more than one speaker. Mr. Samuel Smith said :—

"What India needs is some authentic means of expressing the wishes and feelings of the people, but to get those authentic means it is absolutely necessary that we should concede in some form the principle of representation. I hope from some remarks dropped by the mover of the Address that the principle of representation is to be conceded in this Bill. This is a most essential principle. What we want in India as well as in this country is independent criticism of the action of the Government in India. It is impossible to get this free criticism by means of nominative members. Members nominated by the Government depend upon the Government. Their tenure of office depends upon the Government. My belief is that no measure would tend more to give stability to our rule in India than to graft on our institutions, gradually and wisely, the system of representative government. It is quite impossible that this country can further ignore the educative influences in India. If the Bill which they hoped to see introduced before long carried out the representations of Lord Dufferin, it would go a long way towards satisfying the aspirations of the Indian people."

Mr. Schwann said that he, of course, had not had an opportunity of looking at the provisions of the Bill, but he trusted it contained the elective principle in a more decided form than the measure of 1890. The members of the Indian National Congress did not wish to dogmatise at all in proposing the exact method in which the representation should be provided for. That was left to the Viceroy and the Viceregal Council, but if the Bill was to at all answer the aspirations and wishes of the Indian people it must decidedly contain the representative principle.

Mr. Curzon, Under Secretary of State for India, on behalf of the Government, said that there was every desire to push the Bill forward and carry it into law, adding that he would be out of order were he to discuss the character and provisions of the Bill. He would merely say if it did not in all respects satisfy the expectations of hon. gentlemen opposite it would at any rate meet the definition of being an attempt to deal *honestly* with the question.

The second reading of the Bill was moved in the House of Lords by Viscount Cross on February 15. In his speech he thus alluded to the "Northbrook clause":—

"By a provision introduced by the noble Earl (Northbrook) it enables the Viceroy, with the consent of the Secretary of State, to make certain regulations as to the conditions under which the nominations may be made, and which no doubt gives him a considerable amount of latitude. I am most grateful to the noble Earl (Kimberley) for the remarks that fell from him on the opening night of the Session, and I entirely concur with what he said. Although there has been some delay, one good at any rate has come of it—namely, that those who were anxious for a more advanced measure, have thought the matter well over, and are contented now to approach the subject more tentatively than they were."

The Earl of Kimberley, in the course of a short speech, said:—

"I only wish to make a remark on the subject of great importance dealt with by sub-section 4 of the first clause of this Bill, which enables the Govenor-General in Council, with the approval of the Secretary of State in Council, to make regulations as to the conditions under which nominations shall be made by the Governor-General, Governors, and Lieutenant-Governors respectively, and prescribe the manner in which such regulations shall be carried into effect. It is important and I am bound to say I, in company with my noble friend, would have preferred the phraseology to have been slightly altered so as to make it slightly different in one respect. But at the same time, it is a tentative measure, and, being a tentative measure, must be taken as such. What we really, I think, all desire is that in this matter the Government of India shall be able to exercise their own discretion on the spot upon subjects which they are in a better position to deal with. I think if the Governor-General of India should find he is able to produce in some modified form some system of election, if it should work well, the principle, with the Secretary of State, can be extended if desired. Feeling as I do the great caution that is required in extending this principle to India, I cannot criticise the Bill as it stands in any hostile spirit; and I think it may contain the foundation of a very useful departure in India."

He was followed by the Earl of Northbrook :—

" I agree that the clause to which the Earl has referred will be useful in enabling the Viceroy to popularise in some way the nominations to the Legislative Councils in India. I should have preferred if my noble friend had used the term "representation" instead of "election." It is impossible to express an opinion with any degree of positiveness as to what system will be found to work best in the present condition of India. I think one of the great merits of the Bill is its elasticity. It is my fervent desire myself that some legislation may be passed so that the matter may not stand over again for another year."

The Marquis of Salisbury said :—

" I rise for the purpose of expressing my general assent to the language which has been used by the noble lord. I quite agree with him that the word " representation" better represents the intention we have in view than the more narrow word " election" I desire to correct the idea that this extra representation in the Legislative Councils is to be necessarily confined or even specifically confined to municipal bodies. I do not in the least desire to narrow the language or elasticity of the Bill in the direction of discouraging such bodies; but I must demur to the idea that they must necessarily be the main bodies in India to whom this additional representation must be given. I think we all desire to popularise these bodies and to bring them into harmony with the dominant sympathies of the people. . . . . But we must be careful lest we bring into power not the strong, the vigorous, and the effective, elements of Indian society, but the more artificial and weakly elements which we ourselves have helped to form. It would be a great evil if the strong portion of which the majority in any system of government is composed can under any circumstances be deprived of the share of the government to which they were by their position entitled."

Having passed the House of Lords, the Bill came on for second reading in the Commons on March 28. In his opening speech, Mr. Curzon thus alluded to the elective principle :—

" The hon. member for North Manchester (Mr. Schwann) has placed on the paper an amendment that no reform of these Councils that does not embody the elective principle will be satisfactory. In reply I should like to point out to him that *our Bill does not necessarily exclude some such principle as the method of selection, election, or delegation.* With the permission of the House I will read the words of the sub-section of clause one. It runs as follows : " The Governor-General in Council may from time to time, on the approval of the Secretary of State in Council, make regulations as to the conditions under which such nominations, or any of them, shall be made by the Governor-General, Governors, and Lieutenant-Governors respectively, and prescribe the manner in which such regulations shall be carried into effect." Sir, I will call the attention of the hon. member to that fact. Lord Kimberley himself has elsewhere, in an earlier stage of this Bill, expressed himself as follows : ' I would say in the first place that the clause of the Bill was introduced into the Bill as an amendment by Lord Northbrook, and was received by the Secretary of State with the *avowed object* of giving the Viceroy and the present Governor a considerable latitude in that respect. Lord Kimberley has expressed himself about that clause. He said: ' I am bound to say that I express my whole satisfaction with regard to this elective principle.' And upon another occasion in the present year he said 'I myself believe that under this clause it will be possible for the Governor-General to make arrangements by which certain persons may be present who have been chosen by election by the Governor-General.' *The opinions expressed by Lord Kemberley are those which are shared by the Secretary of State.* Under this Act it would be in the power of the Viceroy to invite representative bodies in India to elect or select or delegate representatives of those bodies or their opinions to be nominated to these Councils and by elective measures. If inquiry be made as to what may be the character of the bodies or associations to which I have alluded I may mention only as an indication of what may be possible, such associations as the association of Zemindars in Bengal, Chambers of Commerce, the municipalities of great cities, the British Indian Association, and perhaps more important than all, the various great religious denominations in the country. I believe the House will hold this method of dealing with the question a wise one. It leaves the initiative to those who are best acquainted with the matter. I cannot conceive anything more unfortunate than that the House should draw up and send out to India a hard and fast electoral system within the four walls of which the Government of that country should confine its views to what some future period should prove inadequate or unsuitable, and that it should have to come back to this House to encounter all the obstacles and delays incidental to Parliamentary vicissitude. . . . The Government believe that the sub-section of Clause 1, which I read out to the House, will provide means by which representatives of the most important sections of native society will be appointed to the Councils, and will be able to expound their views in a higher sense of responsibility than that which they have hitherto felt."

Mr. Schwann then moved his amendment in a weighty speech, which has been published separately. He was immediately followed by Mr. Gladstone, who spoke with no uncertain sound, and whose speech must be quoted in full.

"I commence with a phrase which is not unusual in this House when hon. members say they do not intend to prolong a debate by what they are saying. All I can say is that I should wish if it were in my power to curtail this debate as far as any controversial element in it is concerned. I do not speak of the information and knowledge which we may have from members who are competent to enter into Indian affairs, but as far as controversy is concerned I hope that this debate may on the present occasion be compressed within narrow limits.

"We have before us the Government Bill now proposed for second reading, while my hon. friend the member for Manchester has asked the House by his amendment to declare that in his opinion no reform of the Indian Councils can be satisfactory which does not embody the elective principle. Looking at the Bill and at the amendment I have to ask myself whether there is between them such a differnce of opinion and principle as to make me desirous of going to an issue in respect of that difference. Undoubtedly, looking at the Bill standing by itself I am disposed to agree with my hon. friend that its language is insufficient and unsatisfactory in so far as it is ambiguous. But as against that we have the advantage of an authoritative statement. The Under Secretary has introduced the Bill in a comprehensive and lucid speech, and if I were to criticise any portion of that speech it would be that portion of it in which the hon. gentleman addressed himself to the amendment before the House because it appeared to be his object to put upon the amendment the most hostile construction it would bear. I however, for my part desire to put upon the speeches I have heard and upon the Bill itself the least controversial construction of which they are fairly susceptible. *While the language of the Bill cannot be said to embody the elective principle, it is very peculiar language, unless it is intended to pave the way for the adoption of that principle.* I believe it was suggested by a nobleman in the House of Lords who is friendly to the elective principle in India that, unless it had been intended to leave room for some peculiarities not yet introduced into the Indian system, in the appointment of the members of the Councils under this Bill, it would have been a very singular form of speech to provide not simply that the Governor-General might nominate, but that he might make regulations as to the conditions under which such nominations should be made, eitheir by himself or by the Government in Council. It is plain, I think, we must assume that those who have adopted the language have in their view something beyond mere nomination. Then I come to the speech of the Under Secretary, which distinctly embodies something which I confess appears to me to be not very different from the assertions of my hon. friend, except in that important point that the Under Secretary proposes to leave everything to the discretion, judgment, and responsibility of the Governor-General and the authorities in India. With that limitation I think I may fairly say that the speech of the Under Secretary appears to me to embody the elective principle in the only sense in which we should expect it to be embodied. *My construction of the Under Secretary's speech (I do not think it will admit of any other construction) is that it implies that, in the opinion of the Government and of the House of Lords, a serious effort should be made to consider carefully those elements which in the present condition of India might furnish material for the introduction into the Councils of the elective principle.* If that serious effort in which we are invited to concur is to be made, by whom is it to be made? I do not think that it can be made by the House of Commons except through the medium of empowering provisions. The hon. baronet, the member of Evesham, has spoken at some period of a plan of that kind, and I observed with pleasure the genuinely liberal views of the hon. baronet with respect to Indian affairs and to the Government of the Indian people, and were the hon. baronet to propose a plan of the kind he has indicated to the House it would no doubt contain much that would be useful and wise, and honourable to the spirit of such an assembly as the House of Commons. It may, however, be doubted whether even under such enlightened guidance it would be wise on our part, with our imperfect knowledge, to proceed to the determination of particulars of such a plan.

"I think that the best course to take would be to commend the plan to the authorities in India with a clear indication of the principle on which we desire they should proceed. It is not our business to advise what machinery the Indian Government should use. It is our business to give to those representing Her Majesty's Government in India ample information as to what we believe to be sound principles of government.

"It is also the duty and the function of this House to comment upon any case in which we think the authorities in India have failed to give due effect to those principles, but in the discharge of their high administrative functions, or as to the choice of means, there is no doubt that that should be left in their hands. It would be unwise if we were, with our imperfect knowledge to do anything to embarrass them in the discharge of the duties of an office so highly responsible.

"It is evident that the great question—and it is one of great and profound interest—before the House is that of the introduction of the elective element into the Government of India. That question overshadows and absorbs everything else. It is a question of vital importance, but it is at the same time one of great difficulty. Do not let us conceal from ourselves that no more difficult office has ever been entrusted to a Governor-General than that of administering a Bill such as that which is now before the House in a manner that shall be honourable and wise. I am not disposed to ask of the Governor-General or of the Secretary of State that they shall at once produce large and imposing results. What I wish is that their first step shall be of a genuine nature, and that whatever scope they give to the elective principle shall be real.

"There are, of course, dangers in their way. There is the danger of subserviency. There is another danger, and that is the danger of having persons who represent cliques, classes, or interests, and who may claim the honour of representing India. The old story of the three tailors of Tooley Street does after all embody an important political truth, and it does exhibit a real danger. We must leave it to the wisdom of the Governors-General to do their best to use the most efficient material. What we want is to get at the real heart and mind, the most upright sentiments and the most enlightened thoughts, of the people of India; but it is not an easy matter to do that. I think, however, that upon this point we are justified in being a little more sanguine than the Under Secretary has been in his speech as to he amount of such material.

"I do not, however, venture to indicate where the materials for the elective element in India are to be found. Undoubtedly, as for as my own prepossessions go, I should look presumptively with the greatest amount of expectation and hope to the municipal bodies of India and to the local authorities in which the elective element is already included in that country. What I desire above all is not that there shall be produced at the moment an imposing and magnificent structure, but that there shall be the introduction of that which in itself is in real sympathy with the hearts and minds of the people of India. We cannot judge in what way effect may best be given to the principle, but we must repose just and lengthened confidence in those by whom the government of India has to be administered. My hon. friend in moving the amendment has pointed out authorities in favour of the elective principle, these including men who have been responsible for the actual administration of India. These men, notwithstanding that responsibility, have entirely exempted themselves from whatever prejudicies administration may have entailed on them, and they have distinctly and deliberately sanctioned the introduction of this elective principle. It is there that we stand upon solid ground, and Her Majesty's Government ought to understand that it will be regarded as a most grave disappointment if after all the assurances we have received that an attempt wil be made to bring into operation this powerful engine of government there should not be some result such as we anticipate. *I do not speak of its amount : I speak more of its quality.* In an Asiatic country like India, with its ancient civilisation, with its institutions so peculiar, with such a diversity of races, religions and pursuits, with such an enormous extent of country and such a multitude of human beings as probably, except in China, were never before under a single Government, I can understand that there should be difficulties in carrying what we desire to see accomplished ; but great as the difficulties are the task is a noble task, and will require the utmost prudence and care in conducting it to a successful consummation. But after the assurances we have had from persons of the highest capacity and the greatest responsibity, *I beleve we are justified in looking forward not merely to a nominal but to a real living representation of the people of India.* The great nation to which we belong has undoubtedly had to do most difficult tasks in the government and in the foundation of the institutions of extraneous territories. But all the other parts of the British Empire have presented to us a single problem in comparison with the great problem presented to us by India. Its magnitude, its peculiarity, is such that the task of Great Britain in this respect is far greater than that which any other country has attempted, and far greater than that which it has itself attempted beyond the sea in any of the dependencies of the Empire. I rejoice to think that a great and real advance has been made both before, and especially since, the direct transfer of the Indian Government to the immediate superintendence of the executive at home and to the authority of the Imperial legislature. The progress thus made has been effected by the constant application to the Government of India of the minds of able men acting under a strong sense of political responsibility. All these things induce us to look forward cheerfully to a great future for India, and to expect that a real success will attend the genuine application, even though it may be a limited one, of the elective principles to the government of that vast and almost immeasurable community. If this attempt be sucessful, it will be the accomplishment of a task to which it would be dfficult to find a paralled in history. Under these circumstances. I should deprecate a division of this House on the motion of my hon, friend. I see no such difference between my hon. friend's language and the language of the Bill as ought to induce my hon.

friend to divide the House. If the language of my hon. friend is to receive a perfectly legitimate and not a strained construction, it is only an amplification and not a contradiction of what the speech of the hon. gentleman the Under Secretary implies. I think it would be a great misfortune if the House were to divide on the subject. There is no difference of principle between us. *I think that the acceptance of the elective principle by the hon. gentleman, though guarded was on the whole not otherwise than a frank acceptance.* I do not think there is on that side of the House any jealousy of the introduction into India of that principle which undoubtedly, if it did exist, would form a strong mark of difference between the party which sists there and the party who sit on this side of the House. In reality and in substance we have the same objects in view, and are prepared to recommend the employment of the same means. If that be so, it would be unfortunate that any division should take place, even though the numbers might be very unequal. I certainly could not take part in any division hostile, apparently hostile, to the purposes of the Bill. After the speech of the hon. gentleman such a division would convey a wrong impression. It would be well that the people of India should understand that united views on this question substantially prevail in this House. My persuasion is that those views are united, and that they are such as tend to the development of an enlightened, and not only a liberal but a free system of government. Our desire is that the feeling which has led, as we hope, to the perfect development of free system of government in this country shall be not less apparent in regard to our Asiatic institutions. I venture to submit that the hon. gentleman has no substantial quarrel with the intentions of the Government, and that we should do well to allow this Bill to receive the unanimous assent of the House in the present Session, in the hope that, without serious difficulty, it may shortly become law, and fulfil the beneficent purposes with which it has been framed and submitted to Parliament."

That there was no ambiguity in the mind of the House as to the meaning of these declarations, was at once made apparent by the remarks of the bitterest, perhaps the only bitter, opponent of the Bill, Mr. Maclean. He said:—

"I must say that when the Under Secretary was speaking, and when he read an extract giving the views of Lord Kimberley in the House of Lords, and when I asked him the question whether the Government accepted those views as describing their own intention in bringing forward the Bill, I was somewhat surprised that he should give to that question an unconditional assent.

"Mr. Curzon : I did not say that Lord Kimberley accurately expressed the views of the Government. *On behalf of the Govern-*

ment *I did not dissent from the interpretation put by Lord Kimberley upon the possible application of a clause*:

"Mr. Maclean : I think that amounts to the same thing. The Government does not exclude the principle of election by this Bill. It leaves it in the power of the Governor-General in Council with the approval of the Secretary of State in Council to make regulations under which men shall be chosen on appointment. I think that it is a very dangerous power to be put into the hands of the Secretary of State and the Governor-General for the time being. With all respect to the right hon. gentleman the member for Midlothian (Mr. Gladstone) I maintain that when Parliament is making a great change of this sort it should know exactly what it is doing and that it should not allow the principle of election to be brought in by a side wind. . . . . I think it is absolutely essential that if the principle of election is introduced at all it should have the direct and immediate sanction of both Houses of Parliament, because in that way we may be able to prevent the application of this new system which may be extremely dangerous to our rule out there."

The point was pressed home by Mr. MacNeill, who said :—

" I think the Under Secretary of State will not think me unfair if I ask from him a very deliberate statement. The right hon. gentleman the member for Midlothian (Mr. Gladstone) accepted to the full the statement of the Under Secretary in reference to the admission of the representative principle. These statements were made by the member for Midlothian in presence of the Under Secretary for India, in presence of Lord Cross who was here, and in presence of the leader of the House, and not one of these gentlemen showed the very slightest expression of dissent or disapproval. Then a thick and thin supporter of the Government gets up and accuses the right hon. gentleman the member for Midlothian of taking a tactical advantage of the Indian Government stating that they accepted the principle of representation. Do they accept the principle of representation or do they not ? That would be a very interesting and important question, or is it as the hon. member wishes to infer, that soft words are to be said to the natives of India, and these soft words are to come to no practical advantage? I believe the Government have accepted the representative principle and in that belief I shall accordingly modify my speech."

Sir Richard Temple admitted the recognition of the principle of election or selection so far as to propound a scheme of his own, far more democratic in its way than anything hitherto proposed by Indian reformers. His remarks both support our position and are interesting in themselves; but will be more appropriately considered in India in connection with schemes for carrying the intentions of the Bill into practical effect.

Mr. Curzon, in reply, thus alluded to Mr. Gladstone's speech :—

"I now come to the speech, if I may venture to say so, the wise and weighty speech, with which the right hon. gentleman, the member for Midlothian favoured this House. Undoubtedly, the immediate effect of that speech was to eliminate the element of controversy to a very great extent from our debate this evening, and to diffuse a spirit of harmony over these proceedings. The right hon. gentleman complained, at the outest of his speech, that the language of this Bill was ambiguous, but as he proceeded I was glad to find that the ambiguity was one from which he did not himself draw conclusions hostile to the Bill or its friends. Speaking for the Government, I entirely endorse that part of the right hon. gentleman's speech in which he said it is not for us, not for this House to determine the plan or to devise a machinery, but that the means and initiative must be left in the hands of the Government of India. A subsequent speaker in this debate, the hon. member for Elgin and Nairn (Mr. Seymour Keay) has asked that a mandate should be given from this House. I prefer upon this matter to side with the right hon. gentleman the member for Midlothian. It is the object of the provisions which have been introduced in this Bill and of that particular sub-section of clause 1 which I read to the House, and which has been the subject of so much discussion to-night—to leave the initiative to the Viceroy of India, subject to the assent of the Secretary of State in Council. It will be for him to frame the conditions under which these future nominations may take place. Hon. members have more than once asked to-night whether the words of that clause are to be taken as merely complimentary words. And the hon. member for Elgin and Nairn said he was prepared to stake his political reputation that this clause would be a dead letter. I am sorry to say for the sake of the hon. gentleman that his political reputation stands in very great peril. Undoubtedly these words and this clause were designedly introduced by the Government, and were introduced with a perfectly clear apprehension of their meaning. I do not think there is any want of clearness in the terms in which I expressed the possible application of this clause at an earlier period of the evening, *I endeavoured to give hon. members to understand that this clause was designed to give perfect latitude to the Viceroy in this matter, and that it would admit of the introduction of the principle of representation in India whether the system was election or selection or delegation or whatever the precise method might be that recommended itself to the judgment of the Viceroy.* I think that it was a very important contribution to this debate when the right hon. gentleman the member for Midlothian, speaking with a full knowledge of the enormous responsibilities of Indian government, laid down that the question of the degree and the manner in which this principle is to be carried out, were matters not for the consideration of this House, but primarily for the consideration of the Government of India (a hon. member, "No, No")—I do not think I have misrepresented what the right hon. gentleman said—and that it would be in the highest degree unwise if this House were to endeavour to exercise pressure upon a matter the initiative upon which must necessarily be left to those who are better informed than ourselves. I will not further detain the House. I need only say in conclusion that I entirely accept the statement of the right hon. gentleman as to the objects with which this Bill is introduced. They are undoubtedly to enlist in the service of India what I may describe as the upright sentiment and enlightened opinion of the various sections of native opinion in that great dependency, and if, as the proceedings of this evening appear to show, this Bill will pass without difficulty and with sufficient rapidity into law in the present Session of Parliament, I entertain a certain conviction that it will be attended with very good results."

These admissions and pledges were pressed home in the debate in Committee, when an attempt was made to introduce words distinctly affirming the principle of election. Mr. Schwann said:—

"We are told, sir, that the elective principle is already contained in the Bill; but even with the aid of a powerful microscope I have found it impossible to discover it within the four corners of the Bill. I believe it is supposed to be contained in clause 4, sub-section 1. . . . . Everybody can understand that it will be possible by some arrangement under this sub-section to allow a certain number of men to be elected by large cities or by various bodies to serve on the legislative councils, and that the men thus elected could be nominated by the Viceroy, but it is quite evident that no distinct pledge to this House or to the country is contained in these words, which indeed are considered feeble and impotent by Indian reformers. . . . . I am glad to know that whatever may be the fate of my amendment, some assurances have already been given in this House and 'in another place' which I hope and believe will eventually lead to a large extension of the elective principle. We all know that the hon. gentleman who has charge of the Bill in this House has given repeated assurances as to the intentions of the Government to introduce the elective principle—at any rate not to exclude it. Lord Salisbury in another place gave a general assent to the interpretation which was put by Lord Kimberley on some remarks of Lord Cross who gave considerable latitude to the clause which I have already quoted. . . . . I am glad to think that Lord Salisbury in the remarks which I quoted has made some slight advance from the position taken up by him on a former occasion with regard to Indian reforms. I hope that the 'Black-Man' controversy is closed, and that the noble lord will never again be tempted to use words which, like those, hurt the feelings of a great body of our fellow-subjects in India. I believe he once stated that the idea of election was entirely foreign to the Indian mind and to Indian institutions, and I am glad to know that since then in another place he has taken a broader view of our responsibilities towards India. We have heard some of the assurances given by members of the present Government, and I am glad to think that the right hon. gentleman the member for Midlothian has given us his views upon the elective principle. I will not occupy the time of the House by reading many extracts, but there are a few sentences I should like to quote from his speech on the second reading. . . . . These extracts are important as pledging the action of the future Government of the right hon. member for Midlothian."

Mr. Curzon, in reply, did not withdraw from his former standpoint. He repeated:—" The object of the Government and of the Bill, as I explained in the debate on the second reading, in so far as the elective principle is capable of being received or introduced into the Bill, is to leave the manner, date, and the mode of its introduction absolutely to the Viceroy. We are unable to interfere with his discretion in the matter, and that this is the intention of the Government, and also that it is a wise intention, was recognised by the right hon. gentleman the member for Midlothian himself."

Mr. Bryce, speaking with all the weight of his position in the Liberal Party was equally explicit.

"Therefore, it is certainly desirable to give an independent position, a stronger basis, for an expression of opinion by those members of the Councils. *That, I think, can only be done by having elective members—elected in some form or other. Not only so but it is extremely desirable that the people of India should understand that these members are elected.* It is not only desirable that some members should be elected, but it is also desirable that when they agree with the view the Government takes it should be understood that the agreement is not arrived at because they are nominated members, but as the result of their independent view. The Committee will easily see that the value of an independent opinion is very much diminished if the people do not suppose that they are the genuine opinions of those who express them, but simply the expression of the views of those who are nominated, and who may desire renomination. I do not intend to dwell upon that at length, but I think that the point will be obvious to those who consider what the conditions of India are. For that reason, and for others which it would be tedious to enlarge upon, I think there ought to be some recognition of the elective principle. I believe a great many members of this House, by no means cou-fined to one side of it, desire to see the elective principle largely introduced, and who feel a very strong, and I will say a very confident, hope that under this Bill it will be introduced. We know that the opinions of several very eminent and recent Viceroys are in accordance with that view, and we have, I hope, no reason for thinking that the opinion of the present Viceroy is at variance with theirs. That being so, I for one should be very glad if we had an opportunity of asserting that principle. . . . . I think it was the upshot of the last debate that it would be much better that all matters of detail should be settled by the Indian authorities than that they should be settled in this House. *We have every reason to believe that the Indian authorities desire to settle them in a liberal spirit.* They really possess knowledge we do not possess, and I confess I should be sorry to see passed any amendments which would tie the hands of the Indian Government, and which would force their hands to do that which we believe they have already a desire to do in a generous way. Hon. members will recollect that when the motion was before the House for the second reading a very important declaration was made by the *Under Secretary, who, repeating what had been said in another place, very definitely stated that it would be competent for the Governor-General, if so advised, to introduce the elective principle:* that is to say, there is nothing in the words of the Bill to prevent the Governor-General from doing it. That declaration, which has been practically repeated to-night, was noted at the time by my hon. friend the member for Midlothian, who dwelt upon it, and who said that it left the matter in a very satisfactory way. With that explanation I ask my hon. friend the member for Manchester to withdraw his amendment. Although a division upon it would not prejudice the elective principle, still the effect of it might be to give the impression that this House is not favourable to the principle. I fear, therefore, that the effect of taking the division would leave us in a less advantageous position than we were left in on the second reading. That being so, I cannot help thinking that it would be the best thing to leave the matter in that position, especially after the declaration which the Government have made, that that which has been already adumbrated will be cordially carried out by the Government of India."

Sir Richard Temple had no doubt in the matter. "The Bill leaves the matter in a safe position. *It paves the way for the introduction of the elective principle,* and leaves the responsibility of carrying out the principle with the authorities on the spot."

Subsequently, Mr. Curzon, in declining to add words explicitly affirming the principle of election, distinctly admitted that the Bill was to be read in connection with the debate. He said, "I think the intentions of the Government are clearly defined in the Bill, and have been also clearly stated in the course of these debates. Nobody can be in doubt as to our intentions, and therefore I cannot assent to the proposal to add any further words"

If anything were wanted to confirm this body of evidence, it would be found in the whining of Mr. Maclean. In terror lest the Viceroy should interpret too liberally the mandate of Parliament, he desired to ensure the laying before Parliament (i,e., before a Tory House of Lords) of any scheme prepared by the Indian authorities. In moving an amendment to effect this he said :—

"However, it is now proposed and strongly advocated on the other side of the House that, in order to give expression to public opinion, we should have an elective system of Government in India, and in the present section of the Bill, as finally explained by the Under Secretary, there is no doubt that the elective principle is to be introduced hereafter into the Administration of India. The hon. member has distinctly stated that to be the meaning and intention of the Government. ("No, No.") Well, it is not expressed but it is allowed. . . . . My hon. friend, I think, does not see the full force of the concession he has made to the other side. My own belief is that if we once introduce the elective principle into India, we shall do away with the logical position of our rule in that country. We must be masters there or else we must leave India altogether. If we once admit that the people of that country are entitled, and have the right to the same privileges of self-government that we possess ourselves, then we have no business in India at *all*. Now, it is that strong conviction which compels me to regret very much that the Government should have so far yielded to pressure as to have made that very important concession. I do not understand that it was originally the intention of the Government to do anything of the kind, but Lord Kimberley asked in the House of Lords whether a certain interpretation could not be put on the words of this section, and Lord Cross, with that sprightly amiability which never fails him, said : "Oh, happy thought! Let us adopt the elective principle and introduce it into our Bill." Well, we have the principle, and it is provided that every Secretary of State may make such regulations as he pleases as to the way in which these additional members of the Council should be nominated. . . . . It is to be left absolutely in the power of the Governor-General in Council, with the approval of the Secretary of State, to make as many changes in the constitution of that country as he may desire. I do not say that danger will always arise from the exercise of that authority ; but to use a Johnsonian phrase, the clause contains potentiality of mischief beyond the dreams of the present generation of agitators. *It is obvious that if you have a Governor-General who is anxious to conciliate the people of India, that he will yield one condition after another.* You are yielding to pressure now and are offering thereby an invitation to the people to whom you yield to bring fresh pressure to obtain more that they desire. The Under Secretary, in speaking of this clause, tried to make out really I was attaching exaggerated importance to it. He said it was a very small matter indeed. Well, it is a small matter, no doubt, to some people, if you make a slight breach in the dam of a reservoir by taking away a stone or two, but by such proceeding you may in time desolate the whole of the country below. I think it is a dangerous thing for the Government to have so yielded the scope of the Bill, and *to have given room for the introduction of a great scheme of elective representation in India.*"

But this prophet of evil met with no honour in his own party. Mr. Curzon once more asserted the intentions of the House :—

" But the main ground on which I would ask the House not to accept the amendment is not because of any inherent difficulty, but because of the general grounds on which I have been advocating this Bill and the general principles we have in view. We have persistently taken the line of saying, 'Let us give a broad indication to the Governor-General of the lines on which he may proceed; but we do not desire to hamper him in the smallest degree by any suggestions, much less commands—for this is almost a mandatory amendment—as to what he is to do.' I might in support of that line quote again the speech made a few weeks ago on the second reading by the right hon. gentleman the member for Midlothian (Mr. Gladstone). We desire, as I have had occasion to say over and over again, to leave ample judgment and discretion to the Council; and if we adopt the hon. member's advice—if we introduce in the clause specific reference to the village council—why it alone ?—why not to the other bodies and the other institutions ?—why not to the local boards ?—why not to the municipalities that have been called into existence in India, and which are representatives of a larger area than the village council?—why not to the universities ?—and why not to the branches of the universities ? I might cover a wide field suggesting a number of electoral units which we might indicate in this way to the Governor-General of India. I venture to think that the House will adopt a wiser attitude, will refrain from entering on these particulars, and treat the Government of India in a generous way on those principles of which we have given sufficient indication."

It is not proposed to mar the effect of these weighty pronouncements by any laboured argument. No argument indeed is needed, where the language is so clear and unmistakeable. The object of the Committee is solely to put into the hands of the Indian public a brief composed of irrefragable evidence, on the strength of which they can approach the Government in whose hands the decision has been left, with a claim, to use the words of Mr. Gladstone, "for a real living representation of the people." The evidence is clear on two points. First, the Government of India has the *power* to prepare a scheme of representation more democratic than any the most advanced reformer has dared to suggest. Second, it is expected and believed by Parliament that the Government of India *desires* that its scheme shall be framed in a liberal spirit. Again to use the probing words of Mr. Gladstone, the all-important matter is not of quantity, but of quality. The numbers are, indeed, fewer than we think advisable, but they are fixed probably for some years to come; the strength of the reformers must, therefore, in the immediate future be concentrated on this one object, the endeavour to procure the assent of Government to a scheme which will make the representative element *real and living.*

RULES UNDER THE INDIAN COUNCILS ACT (1892.)

At the meeting of the Viceregal Legislative Council held on the 2nd February 1893, His Excellency the PRESIDENT said :—

" Before we proceed to the business on the paper I should like to make a statement to the Council upon another matter.

" Hon'ble Members will recollect that, during the last session of the Imperial Parliament, a Bill was passed affecting in several respects the Council which I have the honour of addressing, and the local Legislative Councils of Bombay, Madras, Bengal, and the North-West Provinces. The circumstances under which the measure was introduced, and the discussion which took place while it was passing through the two Houses of Parliament, are well known, and I do not think it necessary to recur to them now.

" The changes introduced by the new Act had reference to the constitution of the Legislative Councils, and to their functions. As regards their constitution, the Act provided for an increase in the number of Additional Members, and conferred upon the Governor-General in Council the power of making regulations as to the conditions under which such Members should be nominated. As regards the functions of the enlarged Councils the Act gave them the right of discussing the annual Financial Statement, and also the right of addressing questions to the Government.

" With the object of introducing these changes, it was enacted, under clause I of the new Act, that ' the Governor-General in Council may from time to time, with the approval of the Secretary of State in Council, make regulations as to the conditions under which such nominations,' (*i.e.*, the nominations of Additional Members) ' or any of them, shall be made by the Governor-General, Governors, and Lieutenant-Governors, respectively, and prescribe the manner in which such regulations shall be carried into effect.'

" The provision affecting the functions of the enlarged Councils is clause 2, of the Act, under which ' the Governor-General in Council may from time to time make rules authorising, at any meeting of the Governor-General's Council for the purpose of making Laws and Regulations, the discussion of the annual Financial Statement of the Governor-General in Council and the asking of questions, but under such conditions and restrictions as to subject or otherwise as shall be in the said rules prescribed or declared.'

"The clause contains a like provision authorising the heads of the Local Governments to make similar rules, and it is provided that rules made under the Act by Governors in Council and Lieutenant-Governors shall be 'submitted for, and shall be subject to, the sanction of the Governor-General in Council,' while the rules made by the Govenor-General in Council are to be 'submitted for, and shall be subject to, the sanction of the Secretary of State in Council.'

"Acting upon the lines thus laid down for our guidance in the two clauses which I have quoted, we at once entered into correspondence with the Local Governments with a view to framing regulations under clause I for the nomination of Additional Members. We also prepared rules with regard to the discussion of the Financial Statement and the asking of questions in this Council, and we entered into correspondence with the Local Governments as to the rules which were to be made for similar purposes in the case of their Legislatures.

"The question was one of some difficulty, and necessitated a considerable amount of correspondence. We did not think it necessary to insist upon absolute uniformity as between province and province in the matter of the new rules, but it was obviously desirable that they should be framed in a uniform spirit, and in accordance with what we believed to be the general principles accepted by Parliament when the Act was passed.

"We were able to arrive at an understanding with the Local Governments before the end of the Simla season, and by the end of October last our proposals had been submitted to the Secretary of State.

"It was my earnest hope that we should have obtained the sanction of Her Majesty's Government by a date which would have enabled us to bring the whole of the new rules into operation at the commencement of the present session, but it is scarcely matter for surprise that the Secretary of State should have thought it necessary to examine carefully proposals so far-reaching and so important as those which we have submitted to him, and we learnt a few days ago that, in consequence of a legal difficulty which had been encountered in reference to the new regulations for the appointment of Additional Members, it was not likely that we should, for some little time to come, be made aware of His Lordship's views upon the whole question.

"Under these circumstances we considered it desirable to apply to Her Majesty's Government for permission to introduce immediately that part of the new procedure which has reference to those enlargements of the functions of the Legislative Councils, of which I spoke just now. I am glad to say that this suggestion was readily agreed to by Lord Kimberley, and that we have received his sanction to introduce at once the new rules under which, in future, Hon'ble Members will have the right of discussing our financial proposals, and of addressing questions to us on matters of public interest. The new rules will be published in the official *Gazette*, but it may be desirable that I should take this opportunity of stating briefly what their substance will be, and of mentioning one or two considerations by which we have been guided in framing them.

" The rules for the discussion of the Financial Statement are of the briefest and simplest character. They merely lay down that—

   (i) the Statement shall be explained in Council every year and a printed copy given to each Member ; that

   (ii) after the explanation has been made, each Member shall be at liberty to offer any observations he may wish to make on the Statement : and that

   (iii) the Financial Member shall have the right of reply, and the discussion shall be closed by the President making such observations, if any, as he may consider necessary.

" The rules for the discussion of the Financial Statement in the Local Legislatures are framed upon the same lines, and I need not further refer to them.

" The privilege thus conferred upon the Legislative Councils is, I venture to think, one of great importance. I have, more than once, expressed in this room my strong opinion that the present practice, under which the Council has been allowed an opportunity of criticising the financial policy of the Government of India only upon those occasions when financial legislation was resorted to, could not be defended. The right to criticise the financial administration of a Government is one of which it is impossible to overestimate the value, and I have never concealed my opinion that it was improper as well as illogical that that right should be frequently denied merely upon the technical ground that no Bill upon which a financial debate could be originated happened to be before the Council. The right to discuss, and to criticise, is one which should be either altogether withheld, or altogether conceded. The present arrangement, under which it has been exercised one year and held in abeyance the next, is altogether indefensible. These financial discussions will now take place with regularity, and not upon sufferance, and I feel no doubt that both the public and the Government of India will gain, the one by the wider knowledge and insight into public affairs which it will obtain, the other by the increased opportunity which will be given to it of explaining its position, and defending its policy.

" I will now pass to that portion of the new regulations which has reference to the asking of questions under section 2 of the

Councils Act of last year. The main point which we found ourselves called upon to consider had reference to the conditions and restrictions under which the newly-conferred right should be exercised. We propose that at least six days' notice shall ordinarily be given in writing to the Secretary in the Legislative Department of any questions which an Hon'ble Member intends to ask; but that the President may, if he thinks fit, allow a question to be asked with shorter notice, or may require a longer notice should the circumstances demand it.

"We have laid down that questions must be so framed as to be merely requests for information, and must not be put in an argumentative or hypothetical form, or in defamatory language. No discussion will be permitted in respect of an answer given to a question. These two restrictions are substantially identical with those under which questions may be put to Her Majesty's Government in the British House of Commons. A question, of which notice has been given by one Member, may, if he so desires, be asked by another Member on his behalf.

"There remains one point of the utmost importance. We had to consider whether it was desirable to specify certain subjects with regard to which questions should be inadmissible. It is obvious that there are some matters with regard to which no Government can allow itself to be publicly interpellated, such matters, for example, as military preparations at a time when hostilities are in progress or in contemplation, or matters of financial policy involving the premature disclosure of information affecting the market. The conclusion to which we came was that it was better, at all events in the early days of the new procedure, not to commit ourselves to any such specification of subjects. The impropriety of a question may be due quite as much to the time and circumstances under which it is asked as to the subject-matter, and, although we believe that experience may possibly enable us to lay down rules of the kind suggested, we are of opinion that, for the present, it will be desirable to content ourselves with taking power for the President to disallow a question upon the ground that it cannot be answered consistently with public interests. The reformed Councils will, I have no doubt, show a proper appreciation of the limits within which the right of interpellation can be exercised without injury to public interests, and I have every hope that it will very rarely be found necessary to resort to the veto of the President. I may add that in this case also the rule adopted is similar to that in force in the House of Commons.

"The rules as to questions asked in the Local Legislatures are conceived in the same spirit, but they contain two special and important restrictions. Under the first of these, Members of Council are precluded from asking questions with regard to matters or branches of the administration other than those under the control of the Local Government. The second restriction is this, that in matters which are, or have been, the subject of controversy between the Governor-General in Council, or the Secretary of State, and the Local Government, no question shall be asked except as to matters of fact, while the answer must be confined to a statement of the facts. The necessity of both these restrictions is, I think, so obvious that I need not take up the time of the Council by defending them.

"These are the changes which will come into immediate operation. Of those which are likely to follow, and which affect the constitution, as distinguished from the functions of the Councils, I am obviously precluded from speaking while the matter is still in the hands of the Secretary of State. I will, however, venture to say that, even if the changes which we have been able to introduce were to stop short with those which I have now explained,—and I do not suggest for a moment that this is likely,—a very material advance will have been made in the direction of increasing the usefulness of the Legislative Councils. Their functions have, until now, with the solitary exception to be found in those occasional discussions of the Budget which I have just mentioned, been strictly and narrowly limited to those of assisting the Government of India in the work of legislation. They have been absolutely precluded from asking for information, or inquiring into matters of public interest. In advising Her Majesty's Government to allow us to exceed these limits we feel that we have taken a very serious and far-reaching step. We have taken it under a deep sense of the responsibility which we have assumed; we are fully aware that we are effecting a radical change in the character of these Legislatures; but we are profoundly convinced that the time has come when it is desirable to bring them into closer touch with the rest of the community, and that the reform which we are about to introduce is one which will be for the advantage of the Government as well as of the people of this country.

"I ought, perhaps, to add that the new rules will be published in the *Gazettes* immediately."

CONSTITUTION OF LEGISLATIVE COUNCILS.

AT the meeting of the Viceregal Council held on the 16th March 1893, His Excellency the PRESIDENT said :—

"When, upon a recent occasion, I made a statement to the Council with regard to the procedure to be adopted under the Indian Councils Act of last year, in so far as that procedure had to do with the right of interpellation and of financial discussion, I said that it was out of my power, for the moment, to make any announcement as to the regulations affecting the nomination of Additional Members.

"I am glad to inform the Council that the difficulty which I then mentioned as having prevented the Secretary of State from giving his consent to our proposals, and which I shall presently explain, has been satisfactorily surmounted, and I am now able to tell the Council how the matter stands, both in regard to the Local Councils and in regard to that which I have now the honour of addressing.

"It is, I think, important that we should have a clear idea at the outset of the extent to which these questions have been taken out of our discretion by the terms of the Act, and how far we are free to deal with them by means of the Rules which I am about to lay upon the table.

"In the first place, the maximum number of Additional Members has been, in all cases, fixed by the Act. In Madras and Bombay the present strength is represented by a minimum of 5 and a maximum of 9, including the Advocate-General. Under the Act, there is to be a minimum of 9 and a maximum of 21. The condition laid down in the Act of 1861, that one-half of the Additional Members must be non-officials, still remains in force.

"In the Bengal Legislative Council the present maximum number of Councillors is 12, and this figure is raised by the new Act to 20, subject to the old condition that one-third of the Additional Members must be non-officials.

"In the North-Western Provinces the present strength of Additional Members is 9, and the maximum under the Act is 15, of whom, as in the case of Bengal, one-third must be non-officials.

"These maximum numbers were fixed after much consultation with Her Majesty's Government and with the Local Governments concerned. It is, I think, clear that no one can take upon himself to lay down confidently that, in the case of legislative bodies like these, any one particular number is exactly appropriate. Our communications with the Local Governments, to which I have just referred, disclosed a certain amount of variety of opinion, although the divergence was within comparatively narrow limits. I may, however, say that when the question was first taken up—and Hon'ble Members will recollect that this Bill has been before Parliament for at least three sessions—we found a complete consensus of opinion on the part of all the Local Governments consulted in favour of the view that the Councils might, with advantage, be enlarged, and that it was desirable to increase their authority, and to give them a constitution under which they would be able to afford to the Provincial Governments a larger measure of assistance and support.

" There was another point upon which the consensus of opinion of the Local Governments was equally noticeable. It was felt by all of them that what was desirable was to improve the present Councils rather than to attempt to put in their place bodies comprising a large number of persons, and possessing the attributes of Parliamentary assemblies of the European type. It is a little remarkable that, although the measure was, as I said just now, during three successive sessions before Parliament, no serious attempt was, to the best of my belief, made to substitute largely increased numbers for those which are mentioned in the present Act and in the Bills introduced in preceding sessions.

" Another provision of the Act which requires to be specially considered, in addition to those which have reference to the numbers of the Additional Members, is the provision which has reference to the manner in which they are to be nominated. It is laid down in section I (4) that the "Governor-General in Council may from time to time, with the approval of the Secretary of State in Council, make regulations as to the conditions under which such nominations, or any of them, shall be made by the Governor-General, Governors and Lieutenant-Governors respectively, and prescribe the manner in which such regulations shall be carried into effect.'

" It is under this section the regulations to which I am about to refer have been made.

" Now, it will not escape the attention of the Council that, under the words which I have quoted, the responsibility for these nominations remains with the Governor-General and the heads of the Local Governments concerned, and the Secretary of State, in forwarding the Act to us officially, was careful to point out that ' the ultimate nominating authority still rests with those to whom it was entrusted by the Statute of 1861, and that the responsibility attaching to the careful exercise of this authority by no means diminishes as the number of non-official Members increases, and as the scope of their attributes is enlarged.'

"It was, however, clearly understood, throughout the discussion of the measure, that subject to this ultimate responsibility, the authority upon whom the duty of making the nomination was thus cast should be encouraged to avail himself, as far as the circumstances permitted, of the advice and assistance of any public bodies whose character and position rendered it likely that they could be consulted with advantage. I will read to the Council the words in which this part of the subject was dealt with by the Secretary of State. Writing on the 30th June 1892, he says.—

"It appears to me probable, nevertheless, that the diffusion in the more advanced provinces of education and enlightened public spirit, and the recent organization of local self-government, may have provided, in some instances, ways and means of which the Governments may appropriately avail themselves in determining the character that shall be given to the representation of the views of different races, classes and localities. Where Corporations have been established with definite powers upon a recognised administrative basis, or where Associations have been formed upon a substantial community of legitimate interests, professional, commercial or territorial, Your Excellency and the Local Governors may find convenience, or advantage, in consulting, from time to time, such bodies, and in entertaining at your discretion an expression of their views and recommendations with regard to the selection of Members in whose qualifications they may be disposed to confide.

" There can be no doubt, I think, that the language thus used by the Secretary of State reflected the general feeling on both sides of the British Parliament. It would be easy to multiply quotations, but I will content myself with referring to the important statement made during the course of the debate on the second reading by Mr. Gladstone, who, the Council will remember, was then leader of the Opposition.

" He pointed out that the only reasonable interpretation which could be put upon the clause giving the Governor-General power, not only to nominate Additional Members, but to make regulations as to the conditions under which they were to be nominated, was an interpretation which assumed that something was meant 'beyond mere nomination.' 'The speech of the Under Secretary,' he said, appeared to him ' to embody the elective principle in the only sense in which we should expect it to be embodied. My construction of the Under Secretary's speech is that it implies that a serious effort should be made to consider carefully those elements which, in the present condition of India, might furnish material for the introduction into to the Councils of the elective principle.' Towards the commencement of his speech Mr. Gladstone had pointed out that the proposals of Her Majesty's Government were apparently intended ' to leave everything to the discretion, judgment and responsibility of the Governor-General and the authorities in India,' and, after dwelling upon the difficulty and responsibility of the task, he added: 'I am not disposed to ask of the Governor-General or of the Secretary of State that they shall at once produce large and imposing results. What I wish is that their first steps shall be of genuine nature, and that whatever scope they give to the elective principle shall be real.'

"I should like at this stage to dwell upon the fact that the Government of India, ever since I have the honour of being connected with it, while it has insisted upon the ultimate responsibility of the Government for these nominations, has constantly urged that any Bill which might be passed should render it possible for the Governor-General, and for the heads of the Local Governments, to have recourse to the advice of what, for the want of any more convenient expression, I will describe as 'suitable constituencies.'

"I will venture to quote to the Council an extract from a Despatch sent home by us long ago as the 24th December, 1889, in which we placed on record our opinion that it would be 'well that the measure about to be laid before Parliament should not absolutely preclude us from resorting to some form of election where the local conditions are such as to justify a belief that it might be safely and advantageously adopted.'

"We went on to say that 'we should have been glad if the Bill had reserved to us authority to make rules from time to time for the appointment of Additional Members " by nomination or otherwise," and we should have considered it sufficient if the consent of your Lordship in Council had been made a condition precedent to the validity of such rules. Such an enactment would have provided for the gradual and tentative introduction of a carefully guarded mode of electing Additional Members.'

"I am glad to have had the opportunity of referring to what we said upon this occasion, because I have seen it not unfrequently stated that the Government of India had strenuously opposed the introduction of anything approaching to the elective principle into the Bill, and that we had accepted it reluctantly and under pressure.

"These, then, are the conditions under which we are called upon to frame regulations for the appointment of Additional Members. I think the first observation which it would occur to any one to make would be that, given legislative bodies of the dimensions prescribed for us, or of any dimensions approaching to those laid down in the Act, it would be altogether hopeless to attempt the introduction of a representative system in the sense in which the words are understood in Western communities. How, for instance, would it be possible in a province like that of Bengal, with a population of 70 millions, to allot the handful of seats at our disposal so as to divide the country, either in respect of geographical areas, or in respect of the different communities which inhabit it, in such a manner as to distribute the representation equitably, or to make it really effectual? And I am bound to admit that, to the best of my belief, even those who are credited with opinions of the most advanced type upon Indian political questions have carefully guarded themselves against being supposed to claim for the people of India any system of representation closely imitating the Parliamentary systems of Western Europe.

"We are met, moreover, with this difficulty that, in many parts of India, any system of election is entirely foreign to the feelings and habits of the people, and that, were we to have recourse to such a system, the really representative men would probably not come forward under it.

"Upon a careful review of the whole matter, and of the contents of the Act, as well as of the circumstances under which it had been introduced and passed into law, it appeared to us that the mandate under which we were called upon to act might be summarised in the four following propositions :—

(1) It is not expected of us that we shall attempt to create in India a complete or symmetrical system of representation.

(2) It is expected of us that we shall make a *bonâ fide* endeavour to render the Legislative Councils more representative of the different sections of the Indian community than they are at present.

(3) For this purpose we are at liberty to make use of the machinery of election whatever there is a fair prospect that it will produce satisfactory results.

(4) Although we may to this extent apply the elective principle, it is to be clearly understood that the ultimate selection of all Additional Members rests with the Government, and not with the electors. The function of the latter will be that of recommendation only, but of recommendation entitled to the greatest weight, and not likely to be disregarded except in cases of the clearest necessity.

"It is in this light that the question has been considered and discussed by us with the local Government. We do not believe that the seats placed at our disposal can be distributed according to strict numerical proportion or upon a symmetrical and uniform system. We do not believe, to use Mr. Gladstone's words, that, under the Act, 'large and imposing results' are to be at once obtained, but we do believe that, by having resort to sources other than the unassisted nomination of the Government we shall be able to obtain for these Councils the services of Members who will be in the truest sense representative, but who will represent types and classes rather than areas and numbers.

"We believe that it should not be beyond our power to secure in this manner for the Government the advice and assistance of men connected with different parts of the country, thoroughly aware of the interests and wishes of their countrymen, and able to judge of the extent to which those interests are likely to be affected by any measure of legislation which may be proposed. If we can obtain men of this description, not by selecting them ourselves, but by allowing the great sections of the community a voice in the matter, we believe that the persons selected will bring to our deliberations a very much greater weight of authority than they would have possessed had we been content to rely upon nomination alone.

"It would be impossible for me, within the limits of such a statement as I desire to make this morning, to explain in detail the rules as they will affect each of the four Local Governments concerned. I may say, however, that in each case we have provided by our Rules for the appointment of a number of non-official Additional Members in excess of the minimum determined by the Act, and also that we propose to use at once to the utmost the power of increasing the number of Additional Members in Bengal and the North-Western Provinces, by proclaiming the full maximum allowed under the Act. And I may here explain, in order to avoid misapprehension, what was the nature of the difficulty to which I referred just now, and also upon a former occasion, as having prevented the Secretary of State from at once giving his consent to our scheme as it stood. It was thus : we had proposed that officials should be ineligible for 'election,' or, to use the strictly correct term, for 'recommendation.' A doubt, I believe, arose as to the legality of this exclusion. The legal point was eventually decided in favour of the rule as we had framed it, but, on a full consideration of the case, the Secretary of State in Council came to the conclusion that it was not proper that the whole official class should be subjected to such a disability, and the omission of the rule was consequently proposed by His Lordship and agreed to by us.

"It may, perhaps, interest my hearers if, as an illustration of the manner in which the new Rules will operate, I mention the leading features in the Bengal scheme.

"We have provided that, out of the 20 Councillors who may be nominated under the Act, not more than 10 shall be officials. Under the Act at least one-third of the Additional Members must be non-officials. This would give the Bengal Council 7 unofficial Members. Under the Rules there will be 10, and of these 7 will be nominated by the Lieutenant-Governor on the recommendation of the following bodies and Associations :—

A.—The Corporation of Calcutta ;

B.—Such Municipal Corporations, or group or groups of Municipal Corporations, other than the Corporation of Calcutta, as the Lieutenant-Governor may from time to time prescribe by notification in the *Calcutta Gazette;*

C.—Such District Boards, or group or groups of District Boards, as the Lieutenant-Governor may from time to time prescribe as aforesaid ;

D.—Such Association or Associations of merchants, manufacturers or tradesmen as the Lieutenant-Governor may from time to time prescribe as aforesaid ;

E.—The Senate of the University of Calcutta.

" We have provided that each of the above groups shall (except as hereinafter provided in Rule VII) have at least one Councillor nominated upon its recommendation, but that the Corporation, the Mercantile Associations and the Senate shall have not more than one each.

" It is, however, further provided that the Lieutenant-Governor may nominate to such of the remaining seats as shall not be filled by officials, in such manner as shall, in his opinion, secure a fair representation of the different classes of the community, and that one seat shall ordinarily be held by a representative of the great landholders of the province. It was in our belief absolutely necessary that a part of the seats at our disposal should be reserved in this manner, and filled up by nomination pure and simple. Only by such a reservation was it possible to provide for the representation of those sections of the community which, although sufficiently important to claim a voice in our deliberations, happen to be in a minority, and therefore unable to secure by means of their votes the return of a Member acceptable to themselves. Members thus nominated, although not owing their nomination to the suffrages of their fellow-citizens, will, we hope, be regarded as distinctly representative of the class from which they are taken.

" It is also laid down that it shall be a condition in the case of any person recommended by a Municipal Corporation, or group of Municipal Corporations, that he shall be a person ordinarily resident within the Municipality of the district in which it is situated, or in some one of the Municipalities constituting the group, or of the districts in which they are situated. A similar condition is laid down with reference to persons recommended by District Boards.

"There are other provisions relating to matters of detail, but I do not think it necessary to trouble the Council with them, as the Rules will be published forthwith.

"The Rules for Madras and Bombay, and for the North-Western Provinces and Oudh, differ in some particulars, but are conceived in the same spirit. These also will be published without loss of time.

"It remains for me to say a few words with regard to the manner in which it is proposed to deal with the Council which I have the honour of addressing.

"The Government of India has, from the first, held that the reform of the Viceroy's Council must, to some extent, be dependent upon, and subsequent to, that of the local Councils. It seemed to us that, if the difficulty of obtaining an effectual system of representation was great in the case of the local Councils, it must, *à fortiori*, be greater still in the case of a Council entrusted with the duty of legislating for the whole of India, and, in our belief, the strongest argument in favour of dealing, in the first instance, with the local Legislatures was that we were likely to find in them, when they had been strengthened and reformed, the most convenient electoral bodies for the purpose of choosing a part at all events of the Additional Members who will be appointed to the Legislative Council of the Viceroy.

"This view found much acceptance in Parliament. In his speech in the House of Lords on March 6th, 1890, Lord Northbrook said—'For the present he would not be disposed to go further in respect of the Supreme Council except, perhaps, to allow a selection by each of the subordinate local Legislatures.'

"In the same debate Lord Ripon remarked—That 'he was glad to concur with his noble friend who had just spoken' (Lord Northbrook) 'in the expression of a desire to see the elective or representative element introduced into those Councils. If that step were taken, it would be desirable to introduce the same element into the Council of the Governor-General, very likely in the manner suggested, by selection from the local Councils.'

"We have made a proposal of this kind to the Secretary of State. The maximum number of Additional Members who can be nominated to the Governor-General's Council is 16. Of these at least 8 must, under the Act, be non-officials. We have recommended that there shall be 10 non-officials. We have suggested that 4 of these might be selected and recommended to us by the local Legislatures of the four Provinces having local Councils, that one at least would be required to represent the interests of commerce, and that one might perhaps be chosen from the Calcutta Bar. We propose that the discretion of the Viceroy with regard to the sources from which the remaining 4 might be obtained should be interfered with as little as possible. There may be found in those provinces which do not possess Legislative Councils certain classes and sections of the community so far accustomed to collective action in the promotion of their common interests that they would be qualified to unite in submitting a recommendation in respect of any seat which the Governor-General may desire to fill up from a particular province, and we have been in communication with the Governments of these provinces upon this subject. It is, however, clear that whatever, arrangement may be made with this object should be as elastic as possible. We might for example, find from time to time that the consideration of some particular measure requires the presence in this Council of a Member specially conversant with the subject, or with the territories which the contemplated legislation will affect, and this contingency must certainly be provided for in the case of those provinces which have no local Legislatures, and for which such legislation as is required must be undertaken in the Council of the Governor-General. We do not, therefore, in the case of these provinces see any necessity for such detailed rules for the submission of recommendations as have been proposed for the local Councils. We shall, however, endeavour as far as possible, in the event of a Member being required for this Council from any of the four provinces not having local Councils, to give that Member, by resorting as far as possible to the system of recommendation, a more representative character than would attach to him if he were arbitrarily selected by the head of the Government.

" This is the scheme which, in so far as this Council is concerned, we have submitted to the Secretary of State in terms closely corresponding to those of which I have now made use. We shall at once embody our proposals in a set of rules which will be forwarded for the final sanction of Her Majesty's Government. I have every hope that rules will have been agreed to and will be in operation before the next Calcutta session.

" I have now explained, as far as is necessary, the procedure which will be followed in giving effect to both portions of the Indian Councils Act. It is not unlikely that our proposals will disappoint the expectations of those who would gladly see us travel further and faster along the path of reform. We claim, however, for the changes which we have been instrumental in procuring that they will, beyond all question, greatly increase the usefulness and the authority of these legislative bodies. We are able to show that the number of Additional Members has been materially increased; that we have considerably widened the functions of the Councils by the admission of the right of interpellation and the discussion of the Financial Statement; and, finally, that we shall no longer rely on nomination, pure and simple, for the selection of Additional Members. These are all substantial steps in advance. I hope the Government of India will have the assistance of all concerned in carrying out the Rules in such a way as to secure in the most effectual manner the objects with which they have been framed. It is highly probable that experience will suggest improvements in matters of detail, and I need not say that, in so far as we are not bound by the limits indicated in the Act, we shall be glad to consider the Rules as to some extent experimental and tentative, and that we shall welcome any suggestions which may be offered to us for the purpose of making them work as satisfactorily as possible."

RULES REGARDING THE RECONSTITUTION OF THE LEGISLATIVE COUNCILS OF INDIA.

HOME DEPARTMENT.

PROCLAMATIONS.

PUBLIC.

CALCUTTA, *the 16th March,* 1893.

No. 354.—Whereas, by proclamation issued on the 17th January, 1862, under the provisions of the Act 24 and 25 Vict., Cap. 67 (the Indian Councils Act, 1861), the Governor-General of India in Council extended the provisions of the said Act to the Bengal Division of the Presidency of Fort William in Bengal, and further directed in conformity with the provisions of the said Act that the number of Councillors whom the Lieutenant-Governor of the said Division of the Presidency of Fort William might nominate for his assistance in making Laws and Regulations should be twelve;

And whereas, by section 1 Sub-Section (2), of the Act 55 and 56 Vict., Cap. 14 (the Indian Councils Act, 1892), it was provided that it should be lawful for the Governor-General in Council by proclamation from time to time to increase the number of Councillors whom the said Lieutenant-Governor may nominate for his assistance in making Laws and Regulations, provided that not more than 20 should be so nominated;

It is hereby declared by the said Governor-General in Council that from and after the date of this proclamation, the number of Councillors whom the said Lieutenant-Governor may nominate for the said purpose shall be 20.

No. 355.—Whereas by proclamation issued on the 26th November, 1886, under the provisions of the Act 24 and 25 Vict., Cap 67 (the Indian Councils Act, 1861,) the territories for the time being under the administration of the Lieutenant-Governor of the North-Western Provinces and Chief Commissioner of Oudh were constituted, for the purposes of the said Act, a Province to which the provisions of that Act touching the making of Laws and Regulations should be applicable, and the said Lieutenant-Governor and Chief Commissioner was appointed to be the Lieutenant-Governor of the Province so constituted;

And whereas, by the same proclamation, the Governor-General in Council directed in conformity with the provisions of the said Act that the number of Councillors whom the said Lieutenant-Governor might nominate for his assistance in making Laws and Regulations should be nine;

And whereas by Section 1, Sub-Section (2), of the Act 55 and 56 Vict., Cap 14 (the Indian Councils Act, 1892), it was provided that it should be lawful for the Governor-General in Council by proclamation from time to time to increase the number of Councillors whom the said Lieutenant-Governor may nominate for his assistance in making Laws and Regulations, provided that not more than fifteen should be so nominated.

It is hereby declared by the said Governor-General in Council that from and after the date of this proclamation the number of Councillors whom the said Lieutenant-Governor may nominate for the said purpose shall be fifteen.

NOTIFICATIONS.

PUBLIC.

The 17th March, 1893.

No 359.—The following Regulations, which have been made by the Governor-General in Council under the provisions of Section 1, Sub-Section (4) of the Indian Councils Act 1892, as to the conditions under which nominations of Additional Members of Council shall be made by the Governors of Madras and Bombay and nominations of Councillors by the Lieutenant-Governor of the Bengal Division of the Presidency of Fort William and of the North-Western Provinces and Oudh, respectively, for their assistance in making Laws and Regulations, have received the approval of the Secretary of State for India in Council and are now published for general information:—

Regulations under Section 1 (4) of the Indian Councils Act, 1892, for Madras.

I.—Of the persons, other than the Advocate-General or officer acting in that capacity, to be nominated Additional Members of Council by the Governor of Madras for his assistance in making Laws and Regulations not more than nine shall be officials.

II.—The nominations to seven seats shall be made by the Governor on the recommendation of the following bodies and Associations respectively, namely,—

A.—The Corporation of Madras.

B.—Such Municipal Corporations or group or groups of Municipal Corporations other than the Corporation of Madras as the Governor in Council may from time to time prescribe by Notification in the *Fort St. George Gazette;*

[59]

C.—Such District Boards, or group or groups of District Boards, as the Governor in Council may from time to time prescribe as aforesaid;

D.—Such Association or Associations of merchants, manufacturers or tradesmen as the Governor in Council may from time to time prescribe as aforesaid;

E.—The Senate of the University of Madras:

Provided that the bodies described above under A, B, C, D, and E, respectively, shall each (except as hereinafter provided in Rule VII) have at least one person nominated upon its recommendation, and A, D, and E, not more than one each.

III.—The Governor may, at his discretion, nominate persons to such of the remaining seats as shall not be filled by officials in such manner as shall in his opinion secure a fair representation of the different classes of the community; provided that one seat shall ordinarily be held by a Zemindar paying not less than Rs. 20,000 as *peshkash* annually to Government.

IV.—When a vacancy occurs and is to be filled under Rule II of these Regulations, the Governor shall cause the proper body or group of bodies or Association or Associations to be requested to recommend a person for nomination by the Governor.

V.—The recommendation shall be made—

(a) in the case of a Municipal Corporation or of a District Board, or of the Senate of the University, by a majority of votes of the Corporation, Board, or Senate, respectively;

(b) in the case of Associations not established by law, in the manner laid down in their rules or articles of association for carrying Resolutions or recording decisions upon questions of business brought before the Association;

(c) in the case of a group of Municipal Corporations, District Boards, or Association, by the majority of votes of representatives to be appointed, according to such scale as the Governor in Council may from time to time prescribe, by the Corporations, Boards or Associations.

VI.—It shall be a condition in the case of any person to be recommended by a Municipal Corporation or group of Municipal Corporations that he shall be a person ordinarily resident within the Municipality or the District in which it is situated, or in some one of the Municipalities constituting the group or of the Districts in which they are situated. A similar condition shall also apply to persons to be recommended by District Boards.

VII.—If within two months after receiving the request of the Governor as provided by Rule IV the body or Association or group of bodies or Associations fails to make a recommendation, the Governor may nominate at his discretion a person belonging to the class which the body or Association or group is deemed to represent.

VIII.—If the Governor shall decline to nominate any person who has been, under these Regulations, recommended for nomination, a fresh request shall be issued as provided in Rule IV, and the procedure laid down in Rules V and VII shall apply.

IX.—(a) As soon as conveniently may be after these Regulations come into force, seven of the seats held by non-official persons shall be filled up by recommendation under Rule II.

(b) If there shall not be the full number of seven vacancies available at once for this purpose, the Governor shall determine at his discretion, subject always to the proviso in Rule II, which of the bodies or groups mentioned in that Rule shall be requested to recommend the persons to fill up such vacancies as may then be available; and so whenever and as often as any further vacancies among non-official members become available, until the full number of seven has been completed.

Regulations under Section 1 (4) of the Indian Councils Act, 1892, for Bombay.

I.—Of the persons, other than the Advocate-General or officer acting in that capacity, to be nominated additional Members of Council by the Governor of Bombay for his assistance in making Laws and Regulations not more than nine shall be officials.

II.—The nominations to eight seats shall be made by the Governor on the recommendation of the following bodies and Associations respectively, namely,—

A.—The Corporation of Bombay;

B.—Such Municipal Corporations or group or groups of Municipal Corporations other than the Corporation of the City of Bombay as the Governor in Council may from time to time prescribe by Notification in the *Bombay Government Gazette*;

C.—Such District Local Boards, or group or groups of District Local Boards as the Governor in Council may, from time to time, prescribe as aforesaid;

D.—The Sirdars of the Deccan or such other class of large land-holders as the Governor in Council may, from time to time, prescribe as aforesaid;

E.—Such Association or Associations of merchants, manufacturers or tradesmen as the Governor in Council may, from time to time, prescribe as aforesaid;

F.—The Senate of the University of Bombay:

Provided that the bodies described above under A, B, C, D, E, and F, respectively, shall each (except as hereinafter provided in Rule VII) have at least one person nominated upon its recommendation, and A and F not more than one each.

III.—The Governor may, at his discretion, nominate persons to such of the remaining seats as shall not be filled by officials in such manner as shall in his opinion secure a fair representation of the different classes of the community.

IV.—When a vacancy occurs and is to be filled under Rule II of these Regulations, the Governor shall cause the proper body or group of bodies or Association or Associations to be requested to recommend a person for nomination by the Governor.

V.—The recommendation shall be made—

(a) in the case of a Municipal Corporation or of a District Local Board, or of the Sardars of the Deccan, or such other class of large land-holders as the Governor in Council may, from time to time, prescribe, or of the Senate of the University, by a majority of votes of the Corporation, Board, Body or Senate, respectively;

(b) in the case of Associations not established by law, in the manner laid down in their rules or articles of association for carrying Resolutions, or recording decisions upon questions of business brought before the Association;

(c) in the case of a group of Municipal Corporations, District Local Boards, or Associations, by the majority of votes of representatives to be appointed, according to such scale as the Governor in Council may, from time to time, prescribe, by the Corporations, Boards, or Associations.

VI.—It shall be a condition in the case of any person to be recommended by a Municipal Corporation or group of Municipal Corporations that he shall be a person ordinarily resident within the Municipality or the District in which it is situated or in some one of the Municipalities constituting the group or of the Districts in which they are situated. A similar condition shall also apply to persons to be recommended by District Local Boards.

VII.—If within two months after receiving the request of the Governor as provided by Rule IV, the body or Association or group of bodies or Associations fails to make a recommendation, the Governor may nominate at his discretion a person belonging to the class which the body or Association or group is deemed to represent.

VIII.—If the Governor shall decline to nominate any person who has been, under these Regulations, recommended for nomination, a fresh request shall be issued as provided in Rule IV, and the procedure laid down in Rules V and VII shall apply.

IX.—(a) As soon as conveniently may be, after these Regulations come into force, eight of the seats held by non-official persons shall be filled up by recommendation under Rule II.

(b) If there shall not be the full number of eight vacancies available for this purpose, the Governor shall determine at his discretion, subject always to the proviso in Rule II, which of the bodies or groups mentioned in that Rule shall be requested to recommend the persons to fill up such vacancies as may then be available; and so whenever and as often as any other vacancies among non-official Members become available, until the full number of eight has been completed.

Regulations under Section 1 (4) of the Indian Councils Act, 1892, for Bengal.

I.—The Lieutenant-Governor of Bengal has been authorised by the Proclamation of the Governor-General in Council in the Home Department, No. 354, dated 16th March, 1893, to nominate twenty Councillors for his assistance in making Laws and Regulations. Of these twenty Councillors not more than ten shall be officials.

II.—The nominations to seven seats shall be made by the Lieutenant-Governor on the recommendation of the following bodies and Association respectively, namely:

A.—The Corporation of Calcutta :

B.—Such Municipal Corporations or group or groups of Municipal Corporations other than the Corporation of Calcutta as the Lieutenant-Governor may, from time to time, prescribe by Notification in the *Calcutta Gazette*;

C.—Such District Boards, or group or groups of District Boards, as the Lieutenant-Governor may, from time to time prescribe as aforesaid;

D.—Such Association or Associations of merchants, manufacturers or tradesmen as the Lieutenant-Governor may, from time to time, prescribe as aforesaid;

E.—The Senate of the University of Calcutta :

Provided that the bodies described above under A, B, C, D, and E, respectively, shall each (except as hereinafter provided in Rule VII) have at least one Councillor nominated upon its recommendation, and A. D. and E. not more than one each.

III.—The Lieutenant-Governor may at his discretion nominate persons to such of the remaining seats as shall not be filled by officials in such manner as shall in his opinion secure a fair representation of the different classes of the community; provided that one seat shall ordinarily be held by a representative of the great landholders of the Province.

IV.—When a vacancy occurs and is to be filled under Rule II of these Regulations, the Lieutenant-Governor shall cause the proper body or group of bodies or Association or Associations to be requested to recommend a person for nomination by the Lieutenant-Governor.

V.—The recommendation shall be made—

(a) in the case of a Municipal Corporation or of a District Board, or of the Senate of the University, by a majority of votes of the Corporation, Board, or Senate, respectively;

(b) in the case of Associations not established by law, in the manner laid down in their rules or articles of association for carrying Resolutions or recording decisions upon questions of business brought before the Association;

(c) in the case of a group of Municipal Corporations, District Boards, or Associations, by the majority of votes of representatives to be appointed, according to such scale as the Lieutenant-Governor may from time to time prescribe, by the Corporations, Boards, or Associations.

VI.—It shall be a condition in the case of any person to be recommended by a Municipal Corporation or group of Municipal Corporations that he shall be a person ordinarily resident within the Municipality or the District in which it is situated, or in some one of the Municipalities constituting the group or of the Districts in which they are situated. A similar condition shall also apply to persons to be recommended by District Boards.

VII.—If within two months after receiving the request of the Lieutenant-Governor as provided by Rule IV the body or Association or group of bodies or Associations fails to make a recommendation, the Lieutenant-Governor may nominate at his discretion a person belonging to the class which the body or Association or group is deemed to represent.

VIII.—If the Lieutenant-Governor shall decline to nominate any person who has been, under these Regulations, recommended for nomination, a fresh request shall be issued as provided in Rule IV, and the procedure laid down in Rules V and VII shall apply.

IX.—(a) As soon as conveniently may be after these Regulations come into force, seven of the seats held by non-official persons shall be filled up by recommendation under Rule II.

(b) If there shall not be the full number of seven vacancies available at once for this purpose, the Lieutenant-Governor shall determine at his discretion subject always to the proviso in Rule II, which of the bodies of groups mentioned in that Rule shall be requested to recommend the persons to fill up such vacancies as may then be available; and so whenever and as often as any further vacancies among non-official Councillors become available, until the full number of seven has been completed.

Regulations under Section 1 (4) of the Indian Councils Act, 1892, for the North-Western Provinces and Oudh.

I.—The Lieutenant-Governor of the North-Western Provinces and Oudh has been authorised by the Proclamation of the Governor-General in Council in the Home Department, No. 355, dated 16th March, 1893, to nominate fifteen Councillors for his assistance in making Laws and Regulations. Of these fifteen Councillors not more than seven shall be officials.

II.—The nominations to six seats shall be made by the Lieutenant-Governor on the recommendation of the following bodies and Associations respectively, namely,—

A.—Such Municipal Boards or Committees or group or groups of Municipal Boards or Committees as the Lieutenant-Governor, may, from time to time, prescribe by Notification in the Government *Gazette* for the North-Western Provinces and Oudh;

B.—Such District Boards, or group or groups of District Boards, or Association or Associations of landholders (whether landlords or tenants) as the Lieutenant-Governor may, from to time, prescribe as aforesaid;

C.—Such Associations or Association of merchants, manufacturers or tradesmen as the Lieutenant-Governor may, from time to time, prescribe as aforesaid;

D.—The Senate of the University of Allahabad: Provided that the bodies described above under A, B, C, and D, respectively, shall each (except as hereinafter provided in Rule VII) have at least one Councillor nominated upon its recommendation, and C and D not more than one each.

III.—The Lieutenant-Governor may at his discretion nominate persons to such of the remaining seats as shall not be filled by officials in such manner as shall in his opinion secure a fair representation of the different classes of the community.

IV.—When a vacancy occurs and is to be filled under Rule II of these Regulations, the Lieutenant-Governor shall cause the proper body or group of bodies or Association or Associations to be requested to recommend a person for nomination by the Lieutenant-Governor.

V.—The recommendation shall be made—

(*a*) in the case of a Municipal Board or Committee or of a District Board, or of the Senate of the University, by a majority of votes of the Board, Committee or Senate, respectively;

(*b*) in the case of Associations not established by law, in the manner laid down in their rules or articles of association for carrying Resolutions or recording decisions upon questions of business brought before the Associations;

(c) in the case of a group of Municipal Boards or Committees, District Boards, or Associations, by the majority of votes of representatives to be appointed, according to such scale as the Lieutenant-Governor may, from time to time, prescribe, by the Boards, Committees of Associations.

VI. It shall be a condition in the case of any person to be recommended by a Municipal Board or Committee or group of Municipal Boards or Committees that he shall be a person ordinarily resident within the Municipality or the District in which it is situated, or in some one of the Municipalities constituting the group or of the Districts in which they are situated. A similar condition shall also apply to persons to be recommended by District Boards.

VII. If within two months after receiving the request of the Lieutenant-Governor, as provided by Rule IV the body or Association or group of bodies or Associations fails to make a recommendation, the Lieutenant-Governor may nominate at his discretion a person belonging to the class which the body or association or group is deemed to represent.

VIII. If the Lieutenant-Governor shall decline to nominate any person who has been, under these Regulations, recommended for nomination, a fresh request shall be issued as provided in Rule IV, and the procedure laid down in Rules V and VII shall apply.

IX.—(a) As soon as conveniently may be after these Regulations come into force, six of the seats held by non-official persons shall be filled up by recommendation under Rule II.

(b) If there shall not be the full number of six vacancies available at once for this purpose, the Lieutenant-Governor shall determine at his discretion, subject always to the proviso in Rule II, which of the bodies or groups mentioned in that Rule shall be requested to recommend the persons to fill up such vacancies as may then be available; and so whenever and as often as any further vacancies among non-official Councillors become available, until the full number of six has been completed.

NOMINATION OF REPRESENTATIVES TO SEATS IN THE COUNCIL OF THE LIEUTENANT-GOVERNOR FOR MAKING LAWS AND REGULATIONS ON THE RECOMMENDATION OF PUBLIC BODIES AND ASSOCIATIONS.

RESOLUTION,—JUDICIAL.

Dated Calcutta, the 25th March, 1893.

Under Rule II of the Regulations which have been framed by the Governor-General in Council with the sanction of the Secretary of State under Section I (4) of the Indian Councils Act, 1892, for Bengal, it has been laid down that the nomination to seven seats in the Council of the Lieutenant-Governor for making Laws and Regulations shall be made by the Lieutenant-Governor on the recommendation of the following bodies and associations respectively, *viz,*—

A.—The Corporation of Calcutta;

B.—Such Municipal Corporations or group or groups of Municipal Corporations other than the Corporation of Calcutta as the Lieutenant-Governor may, from time to time, prescribe by Notification in the *Calcutta Gazette*;

C.—Such District Boards, or group or groups of District Boards, as the Lieutenant-Governor may, from time to time, prescribe as aforesaid;

D.—Such Association or Associations of merchants, manufacturers of tradesmen as the Lieutenant-Governor may from time to time prescribe as aforesaid;

E.—The Senate of the University of Calcutta :

Provided that the bodies described above under A, B, C, D, and E, respectively, shall each (except as hereinafter provided in Rule VII) have at least one Councillor nominated upon its recommendation, and A, D, E, not more than one each.

With reference to the above proviso, it has been decided that District Municipalities and District Boards shall each be ordinarily represented by two members.

2. Under Rule V (c) of the same Regulations, it has been laid down that the recommendation of a person for nomination by the Lieutenant-Governor shall be made "in the case of a group of

Municipal Corporations, District Boards, or Associations by the majority of votes of representatives to be appointed according to such scale as the Lieutentnt-Governor may, from time to time, prescribe by the Corporations, Boards, or Associations.

3. The Corporation of Calcutta and the Senate of the University of Calcutta will now be asked by a separate communication to recommend a person for nomination by the Lieutenant-Governor. The votes of the Commissioners of the Corporation of Calcutta will be given at a meeting of the Commissioners. Those of the Fellows of the Senate will be given by voting papers to be delivered personally to the Registrar, or forwarded by post under certain conditions. The Bengal Chamber of Commerce are already represented on the Council by the Vice-President of their body, the Hon'ble Mr. Playfair, and no steps can be taken under clause D of the Rule II above quoted until he resigns his appointment or the term of his office expires.

4. The following observations exclusively refer to the arrangements which will now be made regarding the nomination to the four seats which will be made by the Lieutenant-Governor on the recommendation of District Boards and of Mofussil Municipalities.

5. The Lieutenant-Governor has decided that both district Boards and Municipalities shall be grouped together separately division by division and that the District Boards and Municipalities within each divisional area shall take it in turns to exercise the privilege which is now bestowed on them of recommending a person for nomination to the Council. It is proposed that this privilege should be exercised by the groups of Municipalities and District Boards in each Division according to rotation. The following is a sketch of the form which the rotation may probably assume: but the Lieutenant-Governor cannot bind himself or his successor as to the exact order in which the privilege will in future be exercised:—

Date of election.	Municipalities.	District Boards.
1893	Presidency Division	Patna Division.
	Rajshahye Division	Chittagong Division.
1895	Burdwan Division	Decca Division.
	Orissa Division }	Bhaugulpore Division.
	Chota Nagpore Division }	
1897	Patna Division	Presidency Division.
	Chittagong Division	Rajshahye Division.
1899	Decca Division	Burdwan Division.
	Bhaugulpore Division	Orissa Division.
1901	Presidency Division	Patna Division.
	Rajshahye Division	Chittagong Division.
	and so on.	

The necessary notification will now be published in the *Calcutta Gazette* specifying the groups of District Boards and Municipalities in the Divisions from which a recommendation will be made to the Lieutenant-Governor for the nomination to four seats in Council in 1893.

6. The Lieutenant-Governor is pleased to prescribe the following procedure under which each District Board and Municipality concerned shall, for the purpose of making its recommendation, proceed to elect from amongst its own members an electoral representative who shall be entrusted with full powers to vote for a member to represent the group in Council.

7. In respect of Municipal Corporations, it has been determined that only those Municipalities which enjoy a clear income from Municipal resources proper of Rs. 5,000 and over shall exercise the right of electing an electoral representative. The voting power of each of these representatives will be calculated by the income of the Municipalities concerned according to the following scale:—

		Votes.
Municipalities with an income of Rs. 5,000 and less than Rs. 10,000 will be entitled to	...	1
Municipalities with an income of ,, 10,000 and less than Rs. 20,000	...	2
Municipalities with an income of ,, 20,000 and less than Rs. 50,000 to		3
Municipalities with an income of ,, 50,000 and less than Rs. 1,00,000 to	...	4
Municipalities with an income of ,, 1,00,000 and less than Rs. 1,50,000 to	...	5
Municipalities with an income of ,, 1,50,000 and less than Rs. 2,00,000 to	...	6
Municipalities with an income of ,, 2,00,000 and less than Rs. 2,50,000 to	...	7
Municipalities with an income of ,, 2,50,000 and over to	...	8

Each Municipality will elect one electoral representative only, and this representative shall be entitled to exercise all the votes of the Municipality which he represents.

8. All Districts are considered by the Government to be of approximately equal importance, and each District Board will appoint one representative having one vote.

9. According to the scales above laid down, the following Municipal Corporations and District Boards will now proceed to elect their electoral representatives as follows:—

[69]

Municipalities in the Presidency Division.

District.	Names of Municipality.	Ordinary Municipal Income.* Rs.	Number of votes to be exercised by each representative.
24-Prgns	Cossipur-Chitpur	1,16,260	5
	Maniktollah	41,753	3
	Baranagar	39,040	3
	South Suburbs	47,650	3
	Rajpur	6,908	1
	Joynagar	5,033	1
	South Dum-Dum	7,728	1
	South Barrackpur	11,809	2
	North Barrackpur	11,260	2
	Barasat	8,065	1
	Naihati	15,664	2
	Basirhat	6,285	1
Nuddeah	Krishnagur	24,699	3
	Santipur	25,594	3
	Ranaghat	5,583	1
	Kushtea	6,341	1
Jessore	...Jessore	14,405	2
Khulna	...Khulna	10,976	2
Murshidabad	Berhampur	36,538	3
	Lalbagh	24,320	3
	Jangipur	7,355	1
	Kandi	5,777	1
22			45

District Boards in the Patna Division.

Patna.
Gya.
Shahabad.
Durbhunga.
Chumparun.
Muzufferpur.
Sarun.

District Boards in the Chittagong Division.

Tipperah.
Noakholly.
Chittagong.

---

* The Ordinary Municipal Income is found from Statement II attached to the Resolution on the working of Municipalities in 1891-92, by deducting from head column II the figures shown in head columns 8, 9 and 10, i. e., the Special grants, Miscellaneous and Debt heads.

Municipalities in the Rajshahye Division.

District.	Name of Municipality.	Ordinary Municipal Income.*	Number of votes to be exercised by each representative.
		RS.	
Darjiling	{ Darjiling	94,949	4
	{ Kurseong	8,105	1
Rajshahi	{ Rampur Boalia	19,054	2
	{ Natore	10,909	2
Dinajpur	{ Dinajpur	22,434	3
	{ Pabna	15,252	2
Pabna	...Sarajgunge	15,627	2
Bogra	...Bogra	13,026	2
Rungpur	...Rungpur	22,770	3
Julpaiguri	...Julpaiguri	12,318	2
		10	23

10. Under Rule IV of the Regulations quoted, the Lieutenant-Governor now desires that intimation may be at once communicated by the Commissioners of the Divisions concerned to the Chairman of all the Municipalities and District Boards enumerated in the above lists, requesting them to arrange without delay for the convention of a special meeting of each District Board and Municipality concerned at which one of their members may be elected to represent them for the purpose of recommending the nomination of a member in the Lieutenant-Governor's Council. The name of the electoral representative elected in each must be reported at once by the Chairman of the local body concerned for the information of the Commissioner of the Division.

11. The period of two months which is contemplated under Rule VII of the Regulations as the period within which a recommendation shall be made to the Lieutenant-Governor is hereby declared to run from the date on which the Commissioner of the Division issues his invitation to the Chairman of any Municipality or District Board within the group concerned to elect one of their members to represent them for the purpose of recommending the nomination of a member in the Lieutenant-Governor's Council.

12. As soon as the electoral representatives are elected by the local bodies concerned, they will be called upon by the Commissioner of the Division to meet together on an early and con-

---

* The Ordinary Municipal Income is found from Statement II attached to the Resolution on the working of Municipalities in 1891-92, by deducting from head column II the figures shown in head columns 8, 9 and 10, *i. e.*, the Special grants, Miscellaneous and Debt heads.

venient date with special reference to the limit of time imposed under Rule VII of the Regulations, and at such convenient place as he may specify, for the purpose of electing by a majority of votes a person whom they will recommend to the Lieutenant-Governor to be nominated as a member of the Council. The names of all candidates put forward at such meeting shall be duly proposed by one of the electorial representatives present. The election shall be by ballot, and the person elected must obtain a majority of the votes of the representatives present. If on occasion of the first ballot an absolute majority is not obtained the candidate who obtains the least number of votes shall be withdrawn from the election and another ballot shall then be held for the remaining candidates, and so on until an absolute majority is obtained. The electoral representatives present at this meeting shall elect among themselves a Chairman who shall preside and be responsible for the fair and proper exercise of the ballot vote.

As soon as the election is made, the Chairman of the meeting shall, without delay, report to the Commissioner of the Division the name of the person so elected with the number of votes obtained and any other information which it may appear desirable to communicate, and on behalf of the meeting shall recommend to the Lieutenant-Governor to nominate for Council the person so elected. The Commissioner shall submit the report from the Chairman of the meeting, with any observations he may wish to add, to the Chief Secretary to Government, by whom the recommendations will be submitted to the Lieutenant-Governor.

13. Attention is drawn to the following Rule VI of the Regulations which have been framed by the Governor-General in Council and Secretary of State :—

VI.—It shall be a condition in the case of any person to be recommended by a Municipal Corporation or group of Municipal Corporations that he shall be a person ordinarily resident within the Municipality or the District in which it is situated, or in some one of the Municipalities constituting the group or of the Districts in which they are situated. A similar condition shall also apply to persons to be recommended by District Boards.

Under this rule it is not necessary that persons recommended shall be members of any Municipality or District Board concerned, but they must be ordinarily resident within the division from which the recommendation is made. Subject to this condition the rules declare no limit of qualifications and it is left to the electoral representatives to recommend a person under Rule V (c) according to the majority of their votes.

14. The Lieutenant-Governor is anxious to ensure the success of the operation of the new rules, and with this object has been

careful to provide that all the subsidiary arrangements now sanctioned shall, as far as possible be giving effect to by the local bodies concerned with the minimum official interference. He is confident, however, that District Magistrates will afford any assistance that may be required and do their utmost to facilitate the smooth working of the elections. The experiment now being tried is one of considerable importance, and the arrangements made are necessarily of an experimental character, and will be reconsidered, if experience shows that they required modification.

Ordered that a copy of this Resolution be furnished to all Commissioners for information and guidance and for communication to all the District Boards and Municipalities in their Divisions.

Ordered also that a copy be published in the *Calcutta Gazette*.

Ordered also that a copy be submitted with a covering letter to the Government of India for information.

By order of the Lieutenant-Governor of Bengal,

H. J. S. COTTON,
Chief Secretary to the Government of Bengal.

THE LEGISLATIVE COUNCILS.

BOMBAY SCHEME.

The following notification has been published in a Bombay *Government Gazette* Extraordinary :—

No. 40 of 1893—Legislative Department,

BOMBAY CASTLE, 17th *March*, 1893.

Letter from the Secretary to the Government of India, Home Department, No. 328, dated the 13th March, 1893—Enclosing copy of the Regulations under Section 1, sub-section 4 of the Indian Councils Act, 1892, as approved by the Secretary of State in Council, and requesting that they may be published for general information as having been made by the Governor-General in Council and approved by the Secretary of State in Council.

Resolution :—The Regulations as made by the Governor-General in Council and approved by the Secretary of State in Council under Section 1 (4) of the Indian Councils Act, 1892, for Bombay, should be laid on the editor's table without delay.

2. In accordance with Rule IX, the advice and assistance of certain bodies and Associations, described in Rule II, will be invited at the earliest possible opportunity by His Excellency the Governor with a view to obtaining their recommendations of persons to be nominated by His Excellency the Governor as Additional Members of Council for his assistance in making Laws and Regulations.

(Signed) W. LEE WARNER,
Secretary to Government.

No. 41—LEGISLATIVE DEPARTMENT,

BOMBAY CASTLE, 17th *March*, 1893.

NOTIFICATION.

The Governor in Council is pleased to notify for general information that the following Regulations made by the Governor-General in Council under Section 1 (4) of the Indian Councils Act, 1892, for Bombay have been approved by the Secretary of State in Council :—

I—Of the persons, other than the Advocate-General or officer acting in that capacity, to be nominated Additional Members of

Council by the Governor of Bombay for his assistance in making Laws and Regulations, not more than nine shall be officials.

II—The nominations to eight seats shall be made by the Governor on the recommendation of the following |Bodies and Associations respectively, namely,—

A—The Corporation of Bombay ;

B—Such Municipal Corporations or group or groups of Municipal Corporations other than the Corporations of the City of Bombay as the Governor in Council may from time to time prescribe by notification in the *Bombay Government Gazette.*

C.—Such District Local Boards, or group or groups of District Local Boards, as the Governor in Council may from time to time prescribe as aforesaid ;

D.—The Sardars of the Deccan or such other class of large landholders as the Governor in Council may from time to time prescribe as aforesaid ;

E.—Such Association or Associations of merchants, manufacturers or tradesmen as the Governor in Council may from time to time prescribe as aforesaid ;

F.—The Senate of the University of Bombay ;

Provided that the bodies described above under A, B. C. D E. and F, respectively, shall each (except as hereinafter provided in Rule VII) have at least one person nominated upon its recommendation, and A. and F. not more than one each.

III. The Governor may, at his discretion, nominate persons to such of the remaining seats as shall not be filled by officials, in such manner as shall, in his opinion, secure a fair representation of the different classes of the community.

IV.—When a vacancy occurs and is to be filled under Rule II. of these Regulations, the Governor shall cause the proper Body or group of Bodies, or Associations or Association, to be requested to recommend a person for nomination by the Governor.

V.—The recommendation shall be made—

(a) In the case of Municipal Corporation or of a District Local Board, or of the Sardars of the Deccan, or such other class of large landholders as the Governor in Council may from time to time prescribe, or of the Senate of the University, by a majority of votes of the Corporation, Board, Body, or Senate, respectively.

(b) In the case of Associations not established by law, in the manner laid down in their rules or articles of association for carrying resolutions or recording decisions upon qeustions of business brought before the Association.

(c) In the case of a group of Municipal Corporations, District Local Boards, or Associations, by the majority of votes of representatives to be appointed, according to such scale as the Governor in Council may from to time prescribe, by the Corporations, Boards, or Associations.

VI.—It shall be a condition in the case of any person to be recommended by a Municipal Corporation or group of Municipal Corporations that he shall be a person ordinarily resident within the Municipality of the distrcit in which it is situated or in some one of the Municipalities constituting the group or of the districts in which they are situated. A similar condition shall also apply to persons to be recommended by District Local Boards.

VII.—If within two months after receiving the request of the Governor as provided by Rule IV. the Body or Association or group of Bodies or Associations fails to make a recommendation, the Governor may nominate at his discretion a person belonging to the class which the Body or Association or group is deemed to represent.

VIII.—If the Governor shall decline to nominate any person who has been, under these Regulations, recommended for nomination, a fresh request shall be issued as provided in Rule IV, and the procedure laid down in Rules V, and VII. shall apply.

IX.—(a) As soon as conveniently may be after these Regulations come into force, eight of the seats held by non-official persons shall be filled up by recommendation under Rule II.

(b) If there shall not be the full number of eight vacancies available for this purpose, the Governor shall determine at his discretion, subject always to the proviso in Rule II; which of the Bodies or groups mentioned in that rule shall be requested to recommend the persons to fill up such vacancies as may then be available; and so whenever, and as often as any other vacancies among non-official members become available until the full number of eight has been completed.

By order of His Excellency the Right Hon'ble the Governor in Council.

(Signed) W. LEE WARNER,
Secretary of Government.

THE INDIAN COUNCILS ACT.

The resolution of the Madras Government, Order—dated 12th April 1893, No. 32, Legislative. The Regulations framed under section 1 (4) of the Indian Councils Act, 1892, will be published in the Fort St. George and all District Gazettes in English and the Vernaculars.

2. There are at present (including the Advocate-General) eight additional members of Council. As it has been decided to bring the Council up to its full legal strength, the additional members (including the Advocate-General) will in future number twenty-one and of these at least one-half—that is, eleven must be non-officials. The Council contains at present four official additional members (including the Advocate-General) and four non-officials. There are thus six official and seven non-official vacancies to be filled up.

3. His Excellency the Governor has decided, with reference to Rule II, to fill the non-official seats in the following manner :—

1. Upon the recommendation of A (the Madras Municipal Commission).

2. Upon the recommendation of B (the District Municipalities).

2. Upon the rcommendation of C (the District Boards).

1. Upon the recommendation of D (the Chamber of Commerce, Madras).

1. Upon the recommendation of E (the Senate of the Madras University).

4. The President of the Madras Municipal Commission, the Chairman of the Chamber of Commerce and the Registrar of the University will accordingly be requested to communicate to the Chief Secretary to Government, within two months of the date of receipt by them of this Proceedings, the name of the candidate recommended by the Commission, the Chamber and the Senate, respectively. In this connection the attention of the Chamber of Commerce will be drawn to Rule V (b) which regulates the method in which recommendation should be made.

5. With a view to rendering the system of representation now introduced into the Council as complete as possible, the

[77]

Government has resolved to allow each District Municipality and each District Board to propose a candidate. As there are two seats available for the Municipalities and Boards alike, His Excellency in Council considers that it will be advisable to divide both Municipalities and Boards into two groups—a Northern and a Southern. The Northern group will consist of the districts of Ganjam, Vizagapatam, Godavari, Kistna, Nellore, Kurnool, Bellary, Anantapur, Cuddapah, Chingleput and North Arcot and the Municipalities contained therein. The Southern group will consist of the remaining districts (except Madras) and of the Municipalities contained therein. To the Northern group of Municipalities will be allotted one seat and to the Southern group also one seat; similarly, the Northern and Southern groups of District Boards will each have one seat.

6. As a first step, each Municipality and each District Board must submit, so as to reach the Chief Secretary by the 20th May next, a statement containing two names, of which one will be that of the person whom the Municipality or District Board proposes as candidate for ultimate recommendation to His Excellency the Governor for nomination to the Legislative Council, while the other will be that of the person whom the Municipality or Board intends to appoint as its voting delegate; the voting delegate must always be a member of the Municipality or District Board concerned. In this connection the Government thinks it advisable to draw attention to Rule. VI. A Municipality or Board in the Northern group may propose as a candidate any person resident within the Northern group of districts, and, similarly, a Municipality or Board in the Southern group may propose any person resident in the Southern group of districts. Any person desirous of being nominated to the Legislative Council should submit his name to one of the Municipalities or District Boards in the group wherein he resides.

7. Upon receipts of the said statements, the Chief Secretary will compile therefrom a list containing the names of all the candidates proposed and of all the voting delegates and will circulate it as soon as possible to all the Municipalities and District Boards in the group.

8. At noon on the 17th July next, the voting delegates of the Northern group of Municipalities will assemble at Bezvada and will proceed to elect from among those candidates proposed by the Northern group of Municipalities one person for final recommendation to His Excellency the Governor. The election shall be by ballot and the person elected must obtain a clear majority of the votes of the delegates present and voting. If at the first ballot an absolute majority of the votes of such delegates is not obtained, the ballot shall be repeated until such majority is

obtained. The election must be completed by noon of the 18th July at latest, and the result will be immediately reported to the Chief Secretary to Government by the Collector of Kistna to whom the general superintendence and arrangement of the election will be entrusted. On the same day at noon the voting delegates for the Southern group of Municipalities will meet at Trichinopoly and will in every way conform to the above rules; in the case of this group the Collector of Trichinopoly will be responsible for the proper conduct of the election.

9. Exactly similar rules will guide the election of representatives by the Northern and Southern groups of District Boards, except that in their case the delegates will meet at noon on the 18th July and must complete the election by noon or the 19th idem at latest. It is thought advisable to make this distinction in the dates in order to avoid the chance of the Municipalities and Board of a group electing the same representative.

10. The following Notification will be published in the *Fort St. George Gazette*.

NOTIFICATION.

The Governor in Council is pleased, with reference to Rule II of the Rules made under section 1 (4) of the Indian Councils Act, 1892, to declare that, for the present, one seat in the Legislative Council will be filled upon the recommendation of each of the following groups of Municipalities and District Boards and of the following Association of Merchants :—

(i) The Municipal Councils situated in the districts of Ganjam, Vizagapatam, Godavari, Kristna, Kurnool, Bellary, Anantapur, Cuddapah, North Arcot and Chingleput.

(ii) The Municipal Councils situated in the districts of South Arcot, Salem, Coimbatore, Trichinopoly, Tanjore, Madura, Tinnevelly, Nilgiris, Malabar and South Canara.

(iii) The District Boards of Ganjam, Vizagapatam, Godavari Kistna, Nellore, Kurnool, Bellary, Anantapur, Cuddapah, North Arcot and Chingleput.

(iv) The District Boards of South Arcot, Coimbatore, Trichinoply, Tanjore, Madura, Tinnevelly,, Nilgiris, Malabar, and South Canara.

(v) The Chamber of Commerce, Madras.

(True Extract)

A. BUTTERWORTH,
Ag. Under Secy. to Govt.

THE NEW LEGISLATIVE COUNCILS.
THE N-W. P. SYSTEM.

The orders of Government on the subject of the introduction of the elective principle for the nomination of members of the Legislative Council from the Municipalities and District Boards are published in Saturday's *Gazette*. They are to the following effect :—

Under Section 1 (4) of the Indian Councils Act, 1892, for the North-Western Provinces and Oudh, the Lieutenant-Governor is pleased to prescribe the following groups of Municipal Boards for the purpose of recommending to him two persons for nomination as Councillors for his assistance in making Laws and Regulations at the present time :—

First group.	*Second group.*
Lucknow.	Benares.
Agra.	Allahabad.
Bareilly.	Cawnpore.
Meerut.	Gorakhpur.
Fyzabad.	Muttra.

Under Regulations V (c) of the above Regulations, the Lieutenant-Governor is pleased to prescribe that each of the aforesaid Municipal Boards shall, upon receiving a request under Regulation IV, appoint a representative. The representatives of the first group shall meet at Lucknow, and those of the second group at Allahabad, and shall, on behalf of their respective groups, recommend one person to the Lieutenant-Governor by a majority of their votes. Such person in accordance with Regulation VI shall be ordinarily resident in some one of the Municipalities constituting the group.

Under Regulation II B of the Regulations under section 1 (4) of the Indian Councils Act, 1892, for the North-Western Provinces and Oudh the Lieutenant-Governor is pleased to constitute the undermentioned District Boards as two groups for the purpose of recommending to him two persons for nomination as Councillors for his assistance in making Laws and Regulations at the present time :—

First group	*Second group*
Dehra.	Cawnpore.
Saharanpur.	Fatehpur.
Muzaffarnagar.	Banda.
Meerut.	Hamirpur.
Bulandshahr.	Allahabad.
Aligarh.	Jhansi.
Muttra.	Jalaun.

First group.	*Second group.*
Agra.	Benares.
Farukhabad.	Mirzapur.
Mainpuri.	Jaunpur.
Etawah.	Ghazipur.
Etah.	Ballia.
Bareilly.	Gorakhpur.
Bijnor.	Basti.
Budaun.	Azamgarh.
Moradabad.	Fyzabad.
Shahjahanpur.	Gonda.
Pilibhit.	Bahraich.
Lucknow.	Sultanpur.
Unao.	Partabgarh.
Rae Bareli.	Bara Banki.
Sitapur.	
Hardoi.	
Kneri.	

Under Regulation V (c) of the above Regulations the Lieutenant-Governor is pleased to prescribe that each of the aforesaid District Boards shall upon receiving a request under Regulation IV appoint one representative. The representatives of the District Boards in the first group shall meet at Lucknow : those of the District Boards in the second group shall meet at Allahabad. The representatives shall on behalf of their respective groups recommend a person to the Lieutenant-Governor by a majority of their votes. Such person in accordance with Regulation VI shall be ordinarily resident in some one of the districts constituting the group.

CORRESPONDENCE BETWEEN THE GOVERNMENT OF MADRAS, GOVERNMENT OF INDIA AND THE RIGHT HONORABLE SECRETARY OF STATE.

From C. J. LYALL, Esq, C.I.E., Secretary to the Government of India, Home Department (Public), to the Chief Secretary to the Government of Madras, dated Calcutta, 13th March 1893, No. 327 :—

With reference to the correspondence ending with my letter to your address No. 2137, dated the 27th October 1892, on the subject of the Regulations to be made under section I, sub-section (4), of the Indian Councils Act, 1892, I am directed to enclose for the information of the Governor in Council a copy of a despatch No. 68, dated the 26th October 1892, with which the Government of India forwarded for the approval of the Secretary of State in Council a draft of such regulations for the Legislative Council of His Excellency the Governor of Madras, and of His Lordship's reply No. 24, dated the 16th February 1893, conveying his approval of the draft subject to certain modifications. A copy of the regulations as now approved is also enclosed, and 1 am to request that they may, under the orders of the Governor in Council, be published for general information as having been made by the Governor General in Council and approved by the Secretary of State in Council. They will appear in the next issue of the *Gazette of India*.

2. It will be observed that the regulations now forwarded differ slightly from the draft which accompanied your letter No. 49, dated the 3rd September 1892.

Rule I of that draft followed too closely the wording of the draft proposed for the North-Western Provinces and Oudh, where the number of Councillors has to be fixed by a proclamation issued under section 1, sub-section (2), of the Statute; in Madras sub-section (I) of the same section specifies the number of additional Members of Council who may be nominated, and no proclamation is necessary.

In Rule II it will be observed that "Governor in Council" has been substituted for "Governor" in sub-clauses B, C, and D, and a proviso has been added limiting the number of members to be recommended by the Madras Corporation, the Association or Associations of Merchants, and the Senate of the Madras University, to one each.

In Rule III slight differences of wording will be noticed; it is believed that *peshkash* is a more accurate term for the payments made by great zemindars than "Land Revenue," and the proviso has been so worded that, if one of the recommended seats should be held by a zemindar coming under the description given, the Governor will be at liberty to dispose of the seat thus set free by simple nomination.

In Rule V the Government of India decided upon full consideration to retain the wording of the original draft which accompanied my letter No. 1805, dated the 15th August 1892 : here too it will be observed that "Governor in Council" has been substituted for "Governor."

Rule VII of the original draft has been omitted for the reason stated in paragraph 4 of the despatch from the Secretary of State. Should an official be recommended for nomination by any of the recommending bodies specified in Rule II, it would always be open to the Governor, if he thought that the officer's nomination to the Council was undesirable either because he could not be spared from his duties or for any other reason, to request the body to recommend some other person. If the nomination of an official disturbed the proportion of official to non-official members required by Rule I, the recommendation would have to be rejected unless one of the other official members consented to resign his seat so as to restore the right proportion. If the official were accepted and nominated to the Council, this would give the Governor another nomination which might be filled under Rule III.

Rule IX has been drawn, in accordance with the suggestions at the end of paragraph 5 of your letter of the 3rd September, to provide for the interval which must elapse before the system of nomination by recommendation come fully into force.

3. I am to add that His Excellency the Viceroy proposes, at the meeting of the Legislative Council of the Governor General to be held on the 16th instant, to make a statement explaining the operation of the new rules, and I am to invite thereto the attention of His Excellency the Governor in Council. The principles which should be followed in making nominations have already been fully stated in my letter of the 15th August last and its enclosures, and have now received the approval of the Secretary of State. The Government of India have no doubt that these principles will be carefully observed by His Excellency the Governor of Madras in Council.

4. In connection with the enlargement of the Legislative Councils which has been effected by the Statute of 1892 the Government of India have had under consideration the question whether any travelling allowances should be granted to non-official members of the local Councils when summoned to attend a

Council from a place other than the head-quarters of the Government, and have decided that such members shall receive first-class travelling allowances at the ordinary rates for each journey to and from their homes. Article 1283 of the Civil Service Regulations will be amended accordingly.

ENCLOSURES.

Despatch from the Government of India, Home Department (Public), to the Right Honorable the Secretary of State for India, dated Simla, 26th October 1892, No. 68.

In continuation of our despatch No. 57, dated the 23rd August last, we have now the honour to address Your Lordship in regard to the regulations which should be made, in exercise of the powers conferred upon us by section 1, clause (4), of the Indian Councils Act, 1892, as to nominations to Local Legislative Councils. We are not yet prepared to submit, for Your Lordship's consideration, regulations dealing with the Governor-General's Council, both because we wish, before doing so, to ascertain your views in regard to the draft regulations for Local Councils, which are enclosed in this despatch, and also because we have not yet received replies to all the letters which we addressed to the Provinces having no Legislative Councils of their own. We anticipate no difficulty, however, in framing regulations for the Supreme Council based upon the general principles embodied in the drafts herewith forwarded. As indicated in our letters to Local Governments of the 15th August last, we believe that the Local Legislative Councils, as reconstituted in each Province under the rules now to be made, will afford the best agency by which recommendations for seats in the enlarged Council of the Governor-General for making laws and regulations can be furnished. As regards Provinces not possessing Legislative Councils, the views which we are disposed to hold will be found stated in our letter of the 22nd August, in which those Provinces were consulted.

2. In considering the shape which the regulations should take, we have borne in mind the fact that, although the Act just passed considerably increases the maximum number of additional Members or Councillors who may be summoned to assist the Heads of the Supreme and Local Governments in the task of legislation, the numbers fixed are nevertheless such as altogether to preclude the idea of any detailed and individual representation of the multifarious interests and numerous local divisions of the Indian Empire. We have also kept in view the considerations stated in paragraph 6 of your predecessor's despatch of the 30th June last, that the ultimate nominating authority must still rest with those to whom it was entrusted by the Statute of 1861,

[84]

and that the intention of the Legislature was that " where Corporations have been established with definite powers, upon a recognised administrative basis, or where Associations have been formed upon a substantial community of legitimate interests, professional, commercial, or territorial, the Governor-General and the local Governors might find convenience and advantage in consulting from time to time such bodies and in entertaining at their discretion an expression of their views and recommendations with regard to the selection of members in whose qualifications they might be disposed to confide." We have further given our attention to the opinions expressed in the debates in Parliament when the measure to which effect is now to be given was under discussion. It appears to us that, having in view the numerical limits before referred to and their necessary consequence, and the paramount necessity of giving to all important interests in the country as much representation in the Councils as is possible, the first point for determination is the nature and number of the interests which should be represented. Indian society, from the historical causes to which we need not now refer, is essentially a congeries of widely separated classes, races, and communities, with divergencies of interests and hereditary sentiment which for ages have precluded common action or local unanimity. Representation of such a community, upon such a scale as the Act permits, can only be secured by providing that each important class shall at least have the opprtunity of making its views known in the Council by the mouth of some member specially acquainted with them. Where such a representation can be secured by the common action of any such bodies as are referred to in Lord Cross's despatch, we are prepared to resort to the method of entertaining an expression of their views and recommendations in the manner suggested by him; but outside such bodies it is clearly necessary to reserve the power of nomination by less formal methods for classes which, though of importance in the community, are not in numerical preponderance or are unaccustomed to act together.

3. Accordingly, in consulting the Local Governments on the subject, we first invited their opinion as to the several classes to which representation should be allotted, and then as to the number of non-official seats in the Councils which could be filled on the advice of recommending bodies, and the number which it was necessary to hold in reserve, with the view of redressing any inequality or defect to which the system of recommendation might lead. Your Lordship will observe from the replies enclosed that the general features of the scheme framed by us have been received with unanimous approval by the Governments consulted, and that they agree in considering that it affords a fair basis for giving effect to the intentions of Parliament. We have explained in the letters to the several Provinces that we have designedly

left the rules as elastic as possible in view of the present tentative and experimental stage of the problem, in order that any step which is found to be injudicious may be easily capable for revocation. We hope, however, that we have succeeded in giving to our proposals a form sufficiently definite to secure a satisfactory advance in the representation of the people in our Legislative Councils, and to give effect to the principle of selection, as far as possible, upon the advice of such sections of the community as are likely to be capable of assisting us in that manner.

4. With these preliminary remarks we beg to invite Your Lordship's attention to the drafts*which we enclose. It will be observed that they are all cast in the same mould. We consider it essential that there should be, as at present, an official majority in the Councils; but we have taken measures to restrict the preponderance of officials as much as possible, consistently with that principle. We have provided in the case of each Province that a majority of the non-official seats shall be filled by recommendation; and we have laid it down, in Rule III, that in the case of the remaining seats the Head of the Government shall make his nominations in such a manner as shall secure, in the whole Council, a fair representation of the different classes of the community. In Madras and Bengal it will be observed that the Government consider that the great landholders may most suitably, in accordance with their own sentiments, be represented by a nominated member. The Governments of Bombay and the North-Western Provinces and Oudh are of a different opinion, and have left these seats to be filled by recommendation. In Rule VI we have not thought it expedient for the present to specify any qualification other than that of residence in the case of the Rural and Urban recommending bodies; and in Rule VII we have declared that officials shall not be eligible for recommendation. Your Lordship will observe that the Government of Bombay have called in question the legality of this exclusion. It does not, however, appear to us that the terms of the Act preclude us from prescribing any qualification for nomination to the Councils that may seem expedient, and we are of opinion that the position of an official member is inconsistent with that representative character which we desire to give to the non-official element. Rule IX reserves to the Head of the Government the power of rejection of a peron recommended, which is necessary in view of the responsibility which, as Lord Cross has pointed out, still attaches to the nominating authority for a proper selection of a Member of Council. Rlue X is a rule of temporary application, intended to provide for the time which must elapse before the regulations now proposed come completely into operation.

*Enclosures Nos, 1, 2, 3 and 4.

5. We trust that the regulations now submitted will meet with the approval of Your Lordship in Council, and that that

approval may be signified to us in time to admit of their promulgation by the 1st of January next.

6. With our despatch of the 23rd August we forwarded for Your Lordship's sanction the rules which we had made under section 2 of the Statute for the discussion of the Financial Statement and for asking questions in the Legislative Council of the Governor-General. The rules submitted by the Local Governments fall within our power of sanction; but the consideration of the drafts submitted has led us to think that some improvements are possible in the question rules enclosed in our despatch, and we now forward a revised copy * of those rules to which we solicit Your Lordship's approval.

* Enclosure No. 5.

7. In connection with this subject we beg to invite Your Lordship's attention to paragraph 7 of the letter from the Government of Bombay, and paragraph 11 of that from the Government of the North-Western Provinces and Oudh, in which enquiry is made whether the Council can be summoned for the purpose of a discussion of the Financial Statement, or of giving replies to questions when no legislative work is before it. The question is not one of much practical importance, as, if it is held that the Council cannot meet except for the purpose of making laws and regulations, it will in most cases be easy to arrange for some formal legislative business to be taken in order to admit of the Financial Statement being discussed or questions asked; but we shall be glad to be favoured with Your Lordship's opinion upon the point raised. The decision appears to turn upon the interpretation of the words in section 2 "at any meeting of the Governor-General's Council for the purpose of making laws and regulations." Do the words " for the purpose of making laws and regulations " qualify the word " meeting " or the word " Council ? " In favour of the latter interpretation it may be urged that the " Council for the purpose of making laws and regulations " is merely an extended phrase for what is commonly called the Legislative Council, and would be so understood apart from the language used in the Indian Councils Act, 1861. On the other hand, the earlier Statute does not seem to recognise any separate Legislative Council. The Council is that of the Governor-General or Governor meeting and having additional members for his assistance in making laws. Section 7 and the last words of section 2 of the Act of 1892 have been relied on as showing that the words "for the purpose of making laws and regulations" should be read with "meeting," and the same inference has been drawn from the comma which, in the last sentence of section 9 of the Act of 1861, separates the words "meetings of the Council" from the words "for the purpose of making laws and regulations only."

Draft Regulations under Section 1 (4) of the Indian Councils Act, 1892, for Madras.

I.—Of the persons, other than the Advocate-General or officer acting in that capacity, to be nominated Additional Members of Council by the Governor of Madras for his assistance in making Laws and Regulations not more than nine shall be officials.

II.—The nominations to seven seats shall be made by the Governor on the recommendation of the following bodies and Associations, respectively, namely,—

    A.—The Corporation of Madras;

    B.—Such Municipal Corporations or group or groups of Municipal Corporations other than the Corporation of Madras as the Governor in Council may from time to time prescribe by Notification in the *Fort St. George Gazette*;

    C.—Such District Boards, or group or groups of District Boards as the Governor in Council may from time to time prescribe as aforesaid;

    D.—Such Association or Associations of merchants, manufacturers or tradesmen as the Governor in Council may from time to time prescibe as aforesaid;

    E.—The Senate of the University of Madras:

Proivded that the bodies described above under A, B, C, D, and E, respectively, shall each (except as hereinafter provided in Rule VIII) have at least one person nominated upon its recommendation, and A, D, and E, not more than one each.

III.—The Governor may at his discretion nominate persons to such of the remaining seats as shall not be filled by officials in such manner as shall in his opinion secure a fair representation of the different classes of the community; provided that one seat shall ordinarily be held by a zemindar paying not less than Rs. 20,000 as *peshkash* annually to Government-

IV.—When a vacancy occurs and is to be filled under Rule II of these regulations, the Governor shall cause the proper body or group of bodies or Association or Associations to be requested to recommend a person for nomination by the Governor.

V.—The recommendation shall be made—

    (a) in the case of a Municipal Corporation or of a District Board, or of the Senate of the University, by a majority of votes of the Corporation, Board, or Senate respectively;

    (b) in the case of Associations not established by law, in the manner laid down in their rules or articles of association for carrying resolutions or recording decisions upon questions of business brought before the Association ;

(c) in the case of a group of Municipal Corporations, District Boards, or Associations, by the majority of votes of representatives to be appointed, according to such scale as the Governor in Council may from time to time prescribe by the Corporations, Boards, or Associations.

VI.—It shall be a condition in the case of any person to be recommended by a Municipal Corporation or group of Municipal Corporations that he shall be a person ordinarily resident within the Municipality or the district in which it is situated, or in some one of the Municipalities constituting the group or of the districts in which they are situated. A similar condition shall also apply to persons to be recommended by District Boards.

VII.—No persons actually in the service of Government shall be eligible for recommendation as a representative of any of the bodies or Associations mentioned in Rule II.

VIII.—If within two months after receiving the request of the Governor as provided by Rule IV the body or Association of or group of bodies or Associations fails to make a recommendation, the Governor may nominate at his discretion a person belonging to the class which the body or Association or group is deemed to represent.

IX.—The Governor may reject any recommendation made under these regulations. In case of such rejection, a fresh request shall be issued as provided in Rule IV, and the procedure laid down in Rules V and VIII shall apply.

X.—(a) As soon as conveniently may be after these regulations come into force, seven of the seats held by non-official persons shall be filled up by recommendation under Rule II.

(b) If there shall not be the full number of seven vacancies available at once for this purpose, the Governor shall determine at his discretion, subject always to the proviso in Rule II, which of the bodies or groups mentioned in that Rule shall be requested to recommend the persons to fill up such vacancies as may then be available ; and so whenever and as often as any further vacancies among non-official members become available, until the full number of seven has been completed.

Despatch from the Right Honorable Lord Kimberley, Her Majesty's Secretary of State for India, to His Excellency the Most Honorable the Governor-General of India in Council, dated India Office, London, 16th February 1893, No. 24, Public.

The draft rules for Local Councils which have been prepared in exercise of the powers conferred upon you by section 1, clause 4,

4, of the Indian Councils Act, 1892, and which are forwarded with your letter in the Home Department, No, 68 (Public), of the 26th of October last, have been considered by me in Council.

2. It appears to me that these proposed regulations are in the main well adapted to carry out the intentions of Parliament. There are, however, two points in respect of which some modification is, in my opinion, desirable.

3. The Government of Bombay objected, as you inform me, to the declaration in Rule VII that officials shall not be eligible as representatives of any of the bodies or associations mentioned in Rule II, on the ground that such a declaration is illegal. I am, however, advised by the Law Officers of the Crown that the proposed regulation is not objectionable in law.

4. Nevertheless, having regard to the fact that the provisions for the nomination of additional members to the Councils, which these regulations will bring into force, are new and have not yet been tested in operation, I am unwilling at their first introduction, and before they have been tried, to place any restrictions that are not clearly necessary upon the power of recommendation to be vested in certain bodies or associations. It seems to me preferable to refrain from imposing on the general authority of the several Governors and Lieutenant-Governors a limit which is not required by the Statute, and of which the publication might produce an erroneous impression as to the relations between the official classes and the population of the country at large. I have therefore decided not to sanction this rule.

5. The second point which I would direct the attention of Your Excellency in Council is that the first sentence of Rule IX is unnecessary, the power of nomination being vested by Statute in the Head of the Government. The words " If the Governor (or Lieutenant-Governor) shall decline to nominate any persons who has been, under these regulations, recommended for nomination " should be substituted for that sentence and the first five words of the second.

6. Subject to these modifications I approve the draft regulations for Local Councils which you have prepared.

7. In the last paragraph of your letter you ask my opinion upon the question whether the Council can be summoned for the purpose of a discussion of the Financial Statement, or of giving replies to questions, when no legislative business is before it. I am advised that a meeting of the Council can be summoned only for the purpose of making laws and regulations, and that it cannot legally be summoned for the purpose of merely discussing the Financial Statement or of giving replies to questions at a time when there is no (strictly) legislative business before it.

Regulations under Section 1 (4) of the Indian Councils Act, 1892, for Madras.

I.—Of the persons, other than the Advocate-General ol officer acting in that capacity, to be nominated Additionar Members of Council by the Governor of Madras for his assistance in making Laws and Regulations, not more than nine shall be officials.

II.—The nominations to seven seats shall be made by the Governor on the recommendation of the following bodies and associations, respectively, namely,—

    A.—The Corporation of Madras ;

    B.—Such Municipal Corporations or group or groups of Municipal Corporations other than the Corporation of Madras as the Governor in Council may from time to tim eprescribe by notification in the *Fort St. George Gazette* ;

    C —Such District Boards, or groups of District Boards, as the Governor in Council may from time to time prescribe as aforesaid ;

    D.—Such Association or Associations of merchants, manufacturers or tradesmen as the Governor in Council may from time to time prescribe as aforesaid ;

    E.—The Senate of the University of Madras :

Provided that the bodies described above under A, B, C, D, and E, respectively, shall each (except as hereinafter provided in Rule VII) have at least one person nominated upon its recommendation, and A, D and E not more than one cach.

III.—The Governor may at his discretion nominate persons to such of the remaining seats as shall not be filled by officials in such manner as shall in his opinion secure a fair representation of the different classes of the community ; provided that one seat shall ordinarily be held by a zemindar paying not less than Rs. 20,000 as *peshkash* annually to Government.

IV.—When a vacancy occurs and is to be filled under Rule II of these Regulations, the Governor shall cause the proper body or group of bodies or association or associations to be requested to recommend a person for nomination by the Governor.

V.—The recommendation shall be made—

    (*a*) in the case of a Municipal Corporation or of a District Board, or of the Senate of the University, by a majority of votes of the Corporation, Board, or Senate respectively ;

    (*b*) in the case of associations not established by law, in the manner laid down in their rules or articles o association for carrying resolutions or recording decisions upon questions of business brought before the associations;

(c) in the case of a group of Municipal Corporations, District Boards, or Associations, by the majority of votes of representatives to be appointed, according to such scale as the Governor in Council may from time to time prescribe, by the Corporations, Boards, or Associations

VI.—It shall be a condition in the case of any person to be recommended by a Municipal Corporation or group of Municipal Corporations that he shall be a person ordinarily resident within the Municipality or the district in which it is situated, or in some one of the Municipalities constituting the group or of the districts in which they are situated. A similar condition shall also apply to persons to be recommended by District Boards.

VII.—If within two months after receiving the request of the Governor as provided by Rule IV the body or association or group of bodies or associations fails to make a recommendation, the Governor may nominate at his discretion a person belonging to the class which the body or asssociation or group is deemed to represent.

VIII.—If the Governor shall decline to nominate any person who has been, under these Regulations, recommended for nomination, a fresh request shall be issued as provided in Rule IV, and the procedure laid down in Rules V and VII shall apply.

IX.—(a) As soon as conveniently may be after these Regulations come into force, seven of the seats held by non-official persons shall be filled up by recommendation under Rule II.

(b) If there shall not be the full number of seven vacancies available at once for this purpose, the Governor shall determine at his discretion, subject always to the proviso in Rule II, which of the bodies or groups mentioned in that rule shall be requested to recommend the persons to fill up such vacancies as may then be available ; and so whenever and as often as any further vacancies among non-official members become available, until the full number of seven has been completed.

ORDER—dated 12th April 1893, No. 32, Legislative.

The Regulations framed under section 1 (4) of the Indian Councils Act, 1892, will be published in the Fort St. George and all District Gazettes in English and the Vernaculars.

2. There are at present (including the Advocate-General) eight additional members of Council. As it has been decided to bring the Council up to its full legal strength, the additional mem-

bers (including the Advocate-General) will in future number twenty-one and of these at least one-half —that is, eleven—must be non-officials. The Council contains at present four official additional members (including the Advocate-General) and four non-official. There are thus six official and seven non-official vacancies to be filled up.

3. His Excellency the Governor has decided, with reference to Rule II, to fill the non-official seats in the following manner:—

    1 upon the recommendation of A (the Madras Municipal Commission).
    2   ,,   ,,   ,,   B (the District Municipalities).
    2   ,,   ,,   ,,   C (the District Boards).
    1   ,,   ,,   ,,   D (the Chamber of Commerce, Madras).
    1   ,,   ,,   ,,   E (the Senate of the Madras University).

4. The President of the Madras Municipal Commission, the Chairman of the Chamber of Commerce and the Registrar of the University will accordingly be requested to communicate to the Chief Secretary to Government, within two months of the date of receipt by them of this Proceedings, the name of the candidate recommended by the Commission, the Chamber and the Senate respectively. In this connection the attention of the Chamber of Commerce willbe drawn to rule V (b) which regulates the method in which recommendation should be made.

5. With a view to rendering the system of representation now introduced into the Councils as complete as possible, the Government has resolved to allow each District Municipality and each District Board to propose a candidate. As there are two seats available for the Municipalities and Boards alike, His Excellency in Council considers that it will be advisable to divide both Municipalities and Boards into two groups—a Northern and a Southern. The Northern group will consist of the districts of Ganjam, Vizagapatam, Godavery, Kistna, Nellore, Kurnool, Bellary, Anantapur, Cuddapah, Chingleput and North Arcot and the Municipalities contained therein. The Southern group will consist of the remaining districts (except Madras) and of the Municipalities contained therein. To the Northern group of wunicipalities will be allotted one seat and to the Southern group also one seat; similarly, the Northern and Southern groups of District Boards will each have one seat.

6. As a first step, each Municipality and each District Board must submit, so as to reach the Chief Secretary by the 20th May next, a statement containing two names, of which one will be that

of the person whom the Municipality or District Board proposes as a candidate for ultimate recommendation to His Excellency the Governor for nomination to the Legislative Council, while the other will be that of the person whom the Municipality or Board intends to appoint as its voting delegate; the voting delegate must always be a member of the Municipality or District Board concerned. In this connection the Government thinks it advisable to draw attention to Rule VI. A Municipality or Board in the Northern group may propose as a candidate any person resident within the Northern group of districts, and, similarly, a Municipality or Board in the Southern group may propose any person resident in the Southern group of districts. Any person desirous of being nominated to the Legislative Council should submit his name to one of the Municipalities or District Boards in the group wherein he resides.

7. Upon receipt of the said statements, the Chief Secretary will compile therefrom a list containing the names of all the candidates proposed and of all the voting delegates and will circulate it as soon as possible to all the Municipalities and District Boards in the group.

8. At noon on the 17th July next, the voting delegates of the Northern group of Municipalities will assemble at Bezváda and will proceed to elect from among the candidates proposed by the Northern group of Municipalities one person for final recommendation to His Excellency the Governor. The election shall be by ballot and the person elected must obtain a clear majority of the votes of the delegates present and voting. If at the first ballot an absolute majority of the votes of such delegates is not obtained, the ballot shall be repeated until such majority is obtained. The election must be completed by noon of the 18th July at latest, and the result will be immediately reported to the Chief Secretary to Government by the Collector of Kistna to whom the general superintendence and arrangement of the election will be entrusted. On the same day at noon the voting delegates for the Southern group of Municipalities will meet at Trichinopoly and will in every way conform to the above rules; in the case of this group the Collector of Trichinopoly will be responsible for the proper conduct of the election.

9. Exactly similar rules will guide the election of representatives by the Northern and Southern groups of District Boards, except that in their case the delegates will meet at noon on the 18th July and must complete the election by noon of the 19th idem at latest. It is thought advisable to make this distinction in the dates in order to avoid the chance of the Municipalities and Boards of a group electing the same representative.

10. The following Notification will be published in the *Fort St. George Gazette*:—

NOTIFICATION.

The Governor in Council is pleased, with reference to Rule II of the Rules made under section 1 (4) of the Indian Councils Act, 1892, to declare that, for the present, one seat in the Legislative Council will be filled upon the recommendation of each of the following groups of Municipalities and District Boards and of the following Association of Merchants :—

(i) The Municipal Councils situated in the districts of Ganjam, Vizagapatam, Godávari, Kistna, Nellore, Kurnool, Bellary, Anantapur, Cuddapah, North Arcot and Chingleput.

(ii) The Municipal Councils situated in the districts of South Arcot, Salem, Coimbatore, Trichinopoly, Tanjore, Madura, Tinnevelly, Nilgiris, Malabar and South Canara.

(iii) The District Boards of Ganjam, Vizagapatam, Godavari, Kistna, Nellore, Kurnool, Bellary, Anantapur, Cuddapah, North Arcot and Chingleput.

(iv) The District Boards of South Arcot, Salem, Coimbatore, Trichinopoly, Tanjore, Madura, Tinnevelly, Nilgiris, Malabar and South Canara.

(v) The Chamber of Commerce, Madras.

(True Extract.)

(Signed) A. BUTTERWORTH,
Ag. Under-Secy. to Govt.

RULES.

For the conduct of business at meetings of the Council of the Governor of Fort St. George for the purpose of making laws and regulations under the provisions of the Act of Parliament 24 and 25 Victoria Chap. 67.

MEETINGS.

I. The word Council as used in these rules shall mean the Council of the Governor of Fort St. George assembled for the purpose of making laws and regulations.

The word President as used in these rules shall mean the Governor, or in his absence, the Senior Civil Ordinary member of Council present and presiding.

II. The Governor shall appoint the times and places of meeting of the Council.

III. The President may adjourn, without any discussion or vote, any meeting or business, whether there be a quorum, present or not, to any future day or to any part of the same day.

IV. Notice of all meetings and adjournments shall be given to each member of the Council by the Assistant Secretary.

V. Any business not disposed of at the time of any adjournment shall on the next meeting of the Council take priority of all other business whatever at such next meeting, unless otherwise specially ordered by the Governor.

VI. If at the time appointed for the holding of any meeting or adjourned meeting, as aforesaid, or if at any time after the commencement of business at such meeting there be not present the quorum required by Section 34 of the Indian Council's Act (that is to say, the Governor or some Ordinary member of Council and four or more members of Council) then the members present shall, without proceeding to business of any kind, adjourn until again summoned by the Governor. In such case an entry shall be made in the journal of the Council by the Assistant Secretary of the hour at which the adjournment may have taken place and of the names of the members present.

Quorum Section 34 of the Act.

DISCUSSIONS.

VII. The President shall regulate the course of business at each meeting of the Council, shall preserve order and regularity in the proceedings of the Council, and shall decide all disputed points of order without debate.

VIII. Any Member may notice a violation of order by drawing the attention of the President to it. When a Member is thus addressing the President, any other Member who may be then speaking shall cease until the point of order is settled.

IX. A decision of the President on a point of order shall be heard in silence and shall be final.

X. If two or more Members speak at the same time, the President shall decide which member is entitled to pre-audience, and such decision shall not be open to question.

XI. No Member shall be allowed to speak except upon a question before the Council.

PETITIONS.

XII. Petitions to the Council must relate to some Bill actually under the consideration of the said Council. Every such petition shall be superscribed "To the Governor in Council," and shall be dated and signed by the petitioner or petitioners. It shall be in respectful and temperate language, and shall conclude with a distinct prayer.

XIII. All petitions as aforesaid shall be transmitted to the Assistant Secretary to Government in the Legislative Department.

XIV. The Assistant Secretary shall make an abstract of every petition so received.

XV. If, in the judgment of the Assistant Secretary, the petition be framed in conformity with Rule No. XII, he shall bring the petition under the consideration of the Council by reading the abstract thereof and the prayer or the substance of the prayer of the petiton; where upon such petition shall be dealt with in such manner as the Council may deem proper.

XVI. If, in the judgment of the Assistant Secretary, the petition be not framed in conformity with Rule No. XII, or if he have reason to doubt the authenticity of any signature there to, he shall certify the same on the back of the petition, and shall report the fact to the Council; in which case the petition shall be rejected by the Council, and the reason of such rejection shall be communicated to, and the petition returned to, the petitioner or petitioners.

XVII. Any Member may make a motion upon any petition brought under the consideration of the Council by the Assistant Secretary, and not rejected as afore said. If no motion be made upon such a petition a note of the fact shall be made by the Assistant Secretary on the petition, and it shall be deposited amongs the records of the Council.

XVIII. If a bill be pending peculiarly affecting private interest and any person whose interests are so affected apply by petition to be heard by himself or his Council upon the subject of the bill, an order may be made upon the motion of a Member, allowing the petitioner to be so heard at a stated time, provided the petition be received by the Assistant Secretary before the matter to which the petition relates has been finally disposed of by the Council.

XIX. In no other case or manner shall any stranger be heard by himself or his Counsel. If the petitioner or his Counsel do not appear at such stated time such leave shall lapse.

XX. Any Member may move that the hearing of any petitioner or of his Counsel shall cease if such petitioner or his Counsel be unduly prolix or irrelevant.

BILLS.

XXI. Any member may move at a meeting of the Council for leave to bring in a Bill in accordance with the provisions of section 38 of the Act, provided that three days' previous notice of the title and subject of the Bill have been given to the Assistant Secretary. If the motion be carried in the affirmative, the member shall send the Bill to the Assistant Secretary with a full statemnnt of objects and reasons and any other papers which he may consider necessary.

XXII. The Assistant Secretary will forthwith cause the Bill together with the statement of objects and reasons, to be, printed, and will send a copy for the use of each member.

XXIII. On the day fixed for the introduction of a Bill or on any subsequent day, the principle of the Bill and its general provisions may be discussed. If the question be resolved in the affirmative, the Bill may be referred to a select Committee for report, and, together with the statement of objects and reasons, shall be published in the official Gazette.

XXIV. The publication of a Bill may be suspended until it has been considered by the select Comitee and reported to the Council, if the Council at the time of referring it to the select Committee shall so order.

XXV. A Bill may be sent to the Assistant Secretary when the Council is adjourned, and the Governor may order its publication together with the statement of objects and reasons which accompanies it. In that case it shall not be necessary to move for leave to bring in the Bill, and if the bill be afterwards introduced it shall not be necessary to publish it again.

XXVI. When such period has elapsed from the publication of a Bill as the Council may have ordered, the select Committee shall make a report thereon.

XXVII. Select Committees may be appointed by the Council for any purpose connected with the business of the Council, and may sit and may report on Bills referred for their consideration although the Council is adjourned.

XXVIII. The Assistant Secretary shall cause all reports of Select Committees to be printed, and shall send copies of such for the use of each member. The report and the Bill, or any sections thereof, if altered, shall at the same time be published in the official Gazette.

XXIX. The report of the Select Committee on a Bill shall be taken into consideration by the Council as soon as conveniently may be; but not until a week after the report has been furnished to the Members.

XXX. Any member wishing to propose an amendment affecting the principle or substance of a bill as settled by the Select Committee, shall send the amendment to the Assistant Secretary at least three days before the meeting of the Council at which the bill is to be considered. The Assistant Secretary shall cause every such amendment to be printed, and shall send a copy for the information of each Member.

XXXI. If any amendment be proposed of which notice has not been given, the President shall decide whether such amendment shall be considered by the Council at the meeting at which it is proposed or be deferred to the next following meeting.

XXXII. Amendments shall be considered in the order of the Sections to which they relate.

XXXIII. If no amendment be made by the Council in a bill as settled by the Select Committee, the bill may at once be passed, and sent to the Governor for his assent. If any amendment be made, the bill shall not be passed at the same meeting, but shall be brought forward again to a furture meeting, and may then be passed with or without further amendment.

XXXIV. When it may not be deemed necessary to refer a bill to a Select Committee under Rule XXIII, a day shall be fixed for its consideration by the full Council, provided that such period shall always intervene between the introduction of a bill and its consideration by the whole Council as will admit of its being published for a reasonable length of time.

XXXV. After the passing of a bill, the Assistant Secretary shall revise and complete the marginal notes thereof.

XXXVI. Each bill as finally settled by the Council shall be signed by the President and forwarded immediately to the Governor for his declaration that he assents to or withholds his assent from the same.

XXXVII. The Governor shall communicate his assent or dissent to the Council, by certificate in writing, on the face of the bill, and the bill with such certificate shall be lodged in the records of the Council.

XXXVIII. The Governor shall transmit forthwith an authentic copy of every law or regulation (Section 40 of the Act.) to which he shall have declared his assent to the Governor General; and no such law or regulation shall have validity until the Governor-General shall have assented thereto, and such assent shall have been signified by him to, and published by, the Governor in the Official Gazette.

XXXIX. The fact of the assent or dissent of the Governor-General shall be communicated to the Council by the Governor personally or by letter, and shall be recorded in the Journal of the Council.

XL. The disallowance of any law or regulation by Her Majesty shall in like manner be communicated to, and recorded by, the Council.

XLI. It shall not be competent to any Member of the Council to make any motion upon or otherwise bring under the consideration of the Council, the exercise by Her Majesty, the Governor or the Governor-General, of their prerogative of disallowing a bill by withholding their assent from it.

ORDER OF BUSINESS.

XLII. After the President shall have taken the chair, petitions and other communications received by the Assistant Secretary shall be reported, and notices of bills given by members intending to introduce them. The Council shall then proceed to the disposal of the business left unfinished at the last meeting, unless otherwise specially determined by the President.

XLIII. Strangers may be admitted into the Council Chamber during the sittings of the Council on the order of the President. Application for orders of admission is to be made to the Assistant Secretary.

XLIV. The President, on the motion of any Member, may direct at any time during a sitting of the Council that strangers withdraw.

ASSISTANT SECRETARY TO GOVERNMENT IN THE LEGISLATIVE DEPARTMENT.

XLV. The duties of the Assistant Secretary to Government in the Legislative Department shall be—

1. To take charge of all the records of the Council.
2. To keep the books of the Council.

3. To keep a minute book, in which he shall enter at the time all the proceedings of the Council in the order in which they occur, and the names of the members present thereat.

4. To Superintend the printing of all the papers ordered to be printed.

5. To assist the Council in such manner as they may order, and to assist any member in framing a bill which he proposes to introduce.

6. To write all letters ordered by the Council to be written.

XLVI. It shall be the duty of the ssistant Secretary, after the passing of a bill, to revise and complete the marginal notes thereof.

BOOKS AND RECORDS.

XLVII. A Journal shall be kept, in which all the proceedings of the Council shall be fairly entered.

Journal of Council. The Journal shall be submitted after each meeting to the President thereof for his confirmation and signature and when so signed shall be the record of the proceedings of the Council. The proceedings of each meeting of Council shall be published in the next Official Gazette, after such meeting, or as soon afterwards as can conveniently be arranged.

XLVIII. All documents ordered to be printed or recorded shall be referred to in the journal, and, *Documents how recorded.* after being identified by the signature of the Assistant Secretary on the original documents, shall be kept with the records.

XLIX. A register shall be kept of all petitions received by the Council, in which shall be entered the *Register of petitions* date of receipt by the Assistant Secretary, a general designation of the petitioners, the object of the petition, the manner in which it has been disposed of, and the date of disposal.

Register of letters. L. A register and index of all letters received and despatched shall be kept.

LI. The President for sufficient reasons may suspend any of the foregoing rules.

LI-A. Any bill respecting which no motion has been made in the Council for two years may, by order of the President, be removed from the list of business. (*Passed 23rd November* 1882.)

By Order,

(Signed). JOHN D. MAYNE,

LEGISLATIVE DEPARTMENT, } *Asst. Secy. to Govt,*
MADRAS, 27*th February,* 1863. } *Legislative Department.*

THE MADRAS LEGISLATIVE COUNCIL.

The following notification is published in the *Gazette* of February 14th.

In exercise of the powers conferred upon him by 55 and 56 Vic., c. 14, section 2 (the Indian Councils Act, 1892), and with the sanction of the Governor-General in Council, the Governor in Council has been pleased to make the following rules which are now published for general information :—

I—Preliminary.

Rule 1.—In these rules—

" Council " means the Council of the Governor of Madras for the purpose of making Laws and Regulations.

" President " means the Governor of Madras, or, in his absence, the Senior Civil Ordinary Member of Council present.

" Member" means a Member of the Council, whether Ordinary or Additional.

II—Rules for the discussion of the Financial Statement in the Council.

Rule 2.—The Financial Statement of the Government of Madras shall be explained in Council every year, and a printed copy given to each member.

Rule 3.—After the explanation has been made each member shall be at liberty to offer any observations he may wish to make on the Statement.

Rule 4.—The member who explained the Statement shall have the right of reply, and the discussion shall be closed by the President making such observations, if any, as he may consider necessary.

Rule 5.—The discussion will be limited to those branches of revenue and expenditure which are under the control of the Local Government; and it will not be permissible to enter upon a criticism of Imperial Finance.

III—Rules for asking questions in the Council.

Rule 6.—No question shall be asked or answered in the Council of the Governor, at a meeting of the Council for the purpose of making laws and regulations, as to any matters or branches of the administration other than those under the control of the Governor in Council; and, in matters which are or have been the subject of controversy between the Governor-General in Council or the Secretary of State and the Local Government, no question shall be asked except as to matters of fact, and the answer shall be confined to a statement of facts.

Rule 7.—Except as provided, above, any question may be asked by any member, subject to the following conditions and restrictions.

Rule 8.—A member who wishes to ask a question shall give at least six clear days' notice in writing to the Secretary of the Council, submitting in full the question which he wishes to ask.

Rule 9.—Questions must be so framed as to be merely requests for information, and must not be in an argumentative or hypothetical form or defamatory of any person or section of the community.

Rule 10.—The President may disallow any question without giving any reason therefor other than that in his opinion it cannot be answered consistently with the public interests, and in such case the question shall not be entered in the Proceedings of the Council.

Rule 11.—The President may, if he thinks fit, allow a question to be asked with shorter notice than six days; and may in any case require longer notice if he thinks fit, or extend, if necessary, the time for answering a question.

Rule 12.—When the President has permitted the question to be asked, it shall be entered in the Notice Paper for the day, and questions shall be put in the order in which they stand in the Notice Paper, before any other business is entered upon at the meeting.

Rule 13.—A question shall be read by the member by whom it was framed, or in his absence, if he so desires, by some other member in his behalf and the answer shall be given either by the President or some other member whom he may designate for the purposes.

Rule 14.—The President may rule, at his discretion, that an answer to a question on the Notice Paper, even though the question be not put, shall be given on the ground of public interest.

Rule 15.—No discussion shall be permitted in respect of an answer given to a question asked under these rules.

Rule 16.—The question asked and the answer given to it shall be entered in the Proceedings of the Council.

A. BUTTERWORTH,
Ag. Under-Secy. to Government.

THE VICEREGAL COUNCIL.

The following notification published in the *Gazette of India*, dated 24th June, 1893 :—

NOTIFICATIONS.

Simla, the 23rd June, 1893.

In exercise of the power conferred by section 1, sub-section 4, of the Indian Councils Act, 1892 (55 & 56 Vict., Chap. 14), the Governor-General in Council has, with the approval of the Secretary of State for India in Council, made the following regulations for the nomination of Additional Members of the Council of the Governor-General of India :—

I.—Of the persons to be nominated additional members of Council by the Governor-General for his assistance in making Laws and Regulations not more than six shall be officials.

II.—The nominations to five seats shall be made by the Governor-General on the recommendation of the following bodies respectively, namely,—

A.—The non-official Additional Members of the Council of the Governor of the Presidency of Fort St. George.

B.—The non-official Additional Members of the Council of the Governor of the Presidency of Bombay.

C.—The non-official members of the Council of the Lieutenant-Governor of the Bengal Division of the Presidency of Fort William in Bengal.

D.—The non-official members of the Council of the Lieutenant-Governor of the North-Western Provinces and Oudh.

E.—The Calcutta Chamber of Commerce.

III.—The Governor-General may at his discretion nominate persons to such of the remaining seats as shall not be filled by officials in such a manner as shall appear to him most suitable with reference to the legislative business to be brought before the Council and the due representation of the different classes of the community.

IV.—When a vacancy occurs and is to be filled under Rule II of these Regulations, the Governor-General shall cause the proper body to be requested to recommend a person for nomination by the Governor-General.

[104]

V.—The recommendation shall be made—

(a) in the case of the non-official Additional Members or non-official Members of a Local Council, by a majority of votes of such members ;

(b) in the case of the Calcutta Chamber of Commerce in the manner laid down in the rules of the Chamber for carrying resolutions or recording decisions upon questions of business brought before it.

VI.—It shall be a condition in the case of any person to be recommended by the non-official Additional Members or non-official Members of a Local Council that he shall be a person ordinarily resident within the province for which such Council is appointed.

VII.—If within two months after receiving the request of the Governor-General as provided by Rule IV the body fails to make a recommendation, the Governor-General may nominate at his discretion a person belonging to the province or class which the body is deemed to represent.

VIII.—If the Governor-General shall decline to nominate any person who has been under these regulations recommended for nomination, a fresh request shall be issued as provided in Rule IV and the procedure laid down in Rules V and VII shall apply.

IX. (a) As soon as conveniently may be after these regulations come into force five of the seats held by non-official persons shall be filled up by recommendation under Rule II.

(b) If there shall not be the full number of five vacancies available at once for this purpose, the Governor-General shall determine at his discretion which of the bodies or groups mentioned in Rule II shall be requested to recommend the persons to fill up such vacancies as may then be available, and so whenever and as often as any further vacancies among non-official members become available, until the full number of five has been completed.

LIST OF DISTRICT BOARDS AND MUNICIPALITIES IN THE PRESIDENCY OF MADRAS.

I. Northern Group.

District Boards.	Municipalities.
1. Anantapur	1. Anantapur.
2. Bellary.	1. Adoni. 2. Bellary.
3. Chingleput	1. Conjeeveram.
4. Cuddapah	1. Cuddapah.
5. Ganjam	1. Berhampore. 2. Chicacole. 3. Parlikamidi.
6. Godavery	1. Ellore. 2. Cocanada. 3. Rajahmundry.
7. Kistna	1. Bezwada. 2. Guntur. 3. Masulipatam.
8. Kurnool	1. Kurnool.
9. Nellore	1. Nellore. 2. Ongole.
10. North Arcot	1. Gudiyatum. 2. Tirupati. 3. Vellore. 4. Walajapet.
11. Vizagapatam	1. Anakapallee. 2. Bimlipatam. 3. Vizagapatam. 4. Vizianagaram.
Total... 11.	Total ... 25.

II. Southern Group.

District Boards.	Municipalities.
1. Coimbatore	1. Coimbatore. 2. Erode. 3. Karur.
2. Madura	1. Madura. 2. Palni. 3. Periyakulam. 4. Dindigul.
3. Malabar	1. Calicut. 2. Cannanore. 3. Cochin. 4. Palaghat. 5. Tellicherry.
4. Nilgiris	1. Coonoor. 2. Ootacamund.
5. Salem.	1. Salem. 2. Tirupatur. 3. Vaniyambadi.
6. South Arcot	1. Chidambaram. 2. Cuddalore.
7. South Canara	1. Mangalore.
8. Tanjore	1. Kumbakonam. 2. Mannargudi. 3. Mayaveram. 4. Negapatam. 5. Tanjore.
9. Tinnevelly	1. Palamcottah. 2. Tinnevelly. 3. Tuticorin.
10. Trichinopoly	1. Srirangam. 2. Trichinopoly.
Total ... 10.	Total ... 30.

www.ingramcontent.com/pod-product-compliance
Lightning Source LLC
Chambersburg PA
CBHW020135170426
43199CB00010B/749